Frac Languedoc-Roussillon
Camden Arts Centre

336 PEK

336 RIOS

336 RIVIERES

336 RIVERS

João Penalva

This book was jointly published
by Frac Languedoc-Roussillon, Montpellier, France,
and Camden Arts Centre, London,
on the occasion of the presentation of
João Penalva's work *336 PEK* (336 RIVERS).

Frac Languedoc-Roussillon, La Galerie, 4 rue Rambaud,
34000 Montpellier, France, 6 May to 26 June 1999.
Curator: Ami Barak.

Camden Arts Centre, Arkwright Road, London N.W.3,
16 November 1999 to 16 January 2000.
Director: Jenni Lomax.

336 PEK was produced with the support
of Frac Languedoc-Roussillon, 20 rue de la République,
34000 Montpellier, France.

The exhibition of *336 PEK* at Camden Arts Centre
was supported by Fundação Calouste Gulbenkian (Lisbon),
Fundação Luso-Americana para o Desenvolvimento,
Instituto de Arte Contemporânea / Portuguese Ministry of
Culture, and The Calouste Gulbenkian Foundation (UK).

Camden Arts Centre receives core funding from
London Arts Board and Camden Council.

Design
Rita Lynce, João Penalva and Manuel Rosa

Printed by
Guide – Artes Gráficas, Lda., Lisbon
(Depósito legal 140014/99)

ISBN 1-900470-0-98

	• 01:21:04:20 01:21:07:00
И он спросил:	E a pergunta dele era:
	• 01:21:07:02 01:21:09:06
«Что ты помнишь о своём отце?»	«De que é que te lembras do teu pai?»
	• 01:21:13:02 01:21:15:10
Но вопрос был слишком общим.	Mas isso era demasiado vago.
	• 01:21:16:00 01:21:19:02
Я попросил его задать вопрос по-другому.	Pedi-lhe que reformulasse a pergunta.
	• 01:21:20:10 01:21:22:14
Тогда он спросил:	Então ele perguntou-me:
	• 01:21:23:05 01:21:25:10
«Что ты помнишь о своем отце сейчас?	«De que é que te lembras do teu pai agora?

•
01:21:04:20
01:21:07:00
Et sa question était :

•
01:21:07:02
01:21:09:06
«Quel souvenir gardes-tu
de ton père ?»

•
01:21:13:02
01:21:15:10
Mais c'était trop vague.

•
01:21:16:00
01:21:19:02
Je lui ai demandé de la reformuler.

•
01:21:20:10
01:21:22:14
Alors il m'a demandé :

•
01:21:23:05
01:21:25:10
«Quel souvenir as-tu
de ton père en ce moment ?

•
01:21:04:20
01:21:07:00
And his question was:

•
01:21:07:02
01:21:09:06
"What do you remember
of your father?"

•
01:21:13:02
01:21:15:10
But that was too vague.

•
01:21:16:00
01:21:19:02
I asked him to rephrase it.

•
01:21:20:10
01:21:22:14
So he asked me:

•
01:21:23:05
01:21:25:02
"What do you remember
of your father now?

	• 01:21:26:14 01:21:28:06
Сию минуту.»	Agora mesmo.»
	• 01:21:31:10 01:21:34:14
Я сказал, что помню звук его зажигалки.	Respondi-lhe que me lembrava do som do seu isqueiro.
	• 01:21:35:18 01:21:38:10
Когда он открывал и закрывал её.	A abrir e a fechar.
	• 01:21:38:18 01:21:41:16
Слегка взмахивая рукой.	Com uma sacudidela de mão.
	• 01:21:42:06 01:21:43:12
Перед собой.	Para a frente.
	• 01:21:43:14 01:21:44:12
Всю жизнь была у него эта зажигалка,	Teve este isqueiro toda vida,

•

01:21:26:14
01:21:28:06
En ce moment même.»

•

01:21:26:14
01:21:28:06
Right now."

•

01:21:31:10
01:21:34:14
J'ai répondu que je me souvenais
du bruit de son briquet.

•

01:21:31:10
01:21:34:14
I answered that I remembered
the sound of his lighter.

•

01:21:35:18
01:21:38.10
Quand il l'ouvrait et le fermait.

•

01:21:35:18
01:21:38:10
Opening and closing.

•

01:21:38:18
01:21:41:16
D'un mouvement rapide du poignet.

•

01:21:38:18
01:21:41:16
With a flick of the wrist.

•

01:21:42:06
01:21:43:12
Vers l'avant.

•

01:21:42:10
01:21:43:12
Forwards.

•

01:21:43:14
01:21:44:12
Il a gardé ce briquet toute sa vie,

•

01:21:43:14
01:21:44:12
All his life he had this lighter,

•

01:21:44:14
01:21:47:08

металлическая бензиновая
зажигалка,

um isqueiro de metal,
a gasolina,

•

01:21:47:10
01:21:51:06

и он всегда закрывал её
одним и тем же движением:

e fechava-o sempre
da mesma maneira:

•

01:21:51:22
01:21:55:06

хлопая крышкой едва заметным
взмахом руки.

fazendo fechar a tampa
com um pequeno gesto.

•

01:21:56:14
01:21:59:18

Звук, который получался при этом,
был гораздо заметнее

O som do estalido
era muito maior

•

01:21:59:20
01:22:01:08

взмаха руки.

do que este gesto.

•

01:22:02:22
01:22:06:00

И казалось, что тишина,
наступавшая после этого,

E o silêncio que se lhe seguia

•
01:21:44:14
01:21:47:08
un briquet métallique, à essence,

•
01:21:47:10
01:21:51:06
qu'il fermait toujours
de la même manière :

•
01:21:51:22
01:21:55.06
en rabattant le chapeau
d'un bref mouvement.

•
01:21:56:14
01:21:59:18
Le claquement
était beaucoup plus long

•
01:21:59:20
01:22:01:08
que ce geste.

•
01:22:02:22
01:22:06:00
Et le silence qui suivait

•
01:21:44:14
01:21:47:08
a metal, petrol lighter,

•
01:21:47:10
01:21:51:06
and he always closed it
the same way:

•
01:21:51:22
01:21:55:06
flicking its cover
with a very small gesture.

•
01:21:56:16
01:21:58:18
The clicking sound was much bigger

•
01:21:58:20
01:22:01:08
than this gesture.

•
01:22:02:22
01:22:06:02
And the silence that followed
seemed still part of it.

	• 01:22:06:02 01:22:08:16
была продолжением звука.	parecia fazer ainda parte dele.
	• 01:22:10:04 01:22:11:18
Что я также помню	Que me lembrava também
	• 01:22:11:20 01:22:14:18
запах бензина от зажигалки, окружавший его.	do cheiro a gasolina de isqueiro à sua volta.
	• 01:22:15:02 01:22:17:20
И запах табака в ванной.	E do cheiro a tabaco na casa de banho.
	• 01:22:19:00 01:22:21:18
Я мог бы ответить, что помню его мёртвым.	Podia ter-lhe respondido que me lembrava dele morto.
	• 01:22:22:06 01:22:23:14
В тёмном костюме.	De fato escuro.

•

01:22:06:02
01:22:08:16
semblait encore lui appartenir.

•

01:22:10:04
01:22:14:18
Que je me souvenais aussi
de l'odeur d'essence autour de lui.

•

01:22:06:08
01:22:09:03
That I remembered also
the smell of lighter fluid around him.

•

01:22:15:02
01:22:17:20
Et de l'odeur de tabac
dans la salle de bains.

•

01:22:10:06
01:22:14:18
And the smell of tobacco
in the bathroom.

•

01:22:19:00
01:22:21:18
J'aurais pu répondre
que je me souvenais de lui mort.

•

01:22:15:02
01:22:17:20
I could have answered
that I remembered him dead.

•

01:22:22:06
01:22:23:14
Dans un complet sombre.

•

01:22:19:00
01:22:21:18
In a dark suit.

•

01:22:23:16
01:22:24:20

В гробу. | Num caixão.

•

01:22:24:22
01:22:27:00

С белой ватой в носу. | Com bolas de algodão nas narinas.

•

01:22:27:16
01:22:30:06

С ватой,
торчащей из одной ноздри. | Um bocado de algodão
a sair-lhe do nariz.

•

01:22:31:06
01:22:34:02

Его волосы причёсаны по-другому, | A risca do cabelo

•

01:22:34:22
01:22:37:06

не так, как он сам их причёсывал, | diferente da que ele usava,

•

01:22:23:16
01:22:24:20
Dans un cercueil.

•

01:22:24:22
01:22:27:00
Des boules de coton
dans les narines.

•

01:22:27:16
01:22:30:06
Un bout de coton
dépassant de son nez.

•

01:22:31:06
01:22:34:02
Sa raie coiffée d'une manière

•

01:22:34:22
01:22:37:06
qui n'était pas la sienne,

•

01:22:22:06
01:22:23:14
In a coffin.

•

01:22:23:16
01:22:24:20
With white cotton wool

•

01:22:24:22
01:22:27:00
in his nostrils.

•

01:22:27:16
01:22:30:06
One bit of cotton
sticking out of his nose.

•

01:22:31:06
01:22:34:02
His hair parted somehow differently

•

01:22:34:22
01:22:37:06
from the way he did it himself,

кем-то, кто, может быть,
его не знал.

•

01:22:38:04
01:22:41:12
feita por alguém que
provavelmente não o conhecia.

Если бы мне задали
тот же вопрос

•

01:22:46:02
01:22:48:14
Tivessem-me
feito esta mesma pergunta

минутой, секундой
раньше или позже,

•

01:22:48:20
01:22:52:02
um minuto, um segundo
antes ou depois,

я ответил бы,
представив иной образ,

•

01:22:52:08
01:22:55:12
teria respondido
com outra imagem,

из другой части фильма,

•

01:22:56:04
01:22:58:08
de outra parte do filme

мелькающего в затаённом
кино в моей голове.

•

01:22:58:10
01:23:01:02
projectado no cinema secreto
da minha cabeça.

•

01:22:38:04
01:22:41:12
par quelqu'un qui ne le connaissait
probablement pas.

•

01:22:46:02
01:22:48:14
Si cette même question
m'avait été posée

•

01:22:48:20
01:22:52:02
une minute, une seconde,
avant ou après,

•

01:22:52:08
01:22:55:12
j'aurais répondu
avec une autre image,

•

01:22:56:04
01:22:58:08
d'un autre moment du film

•

01:22:58:10
01:23:01:02
projeté dans le cinéma secret
de ma tête.

•

01:22:38:04
01:22:41:08
by someone
who probably didn't know him.

•

01:22:46:02
01:22:48:14
Had I been asked
the same question

•

01:22:48:20
01:22:52:02
one minute, one second,
earlier or later,

•

01:22:52:08
01:22:55:12
I would have answered
with another image,

•

01:22:56:04
01:22:57:18
from another part of the film

•

01:22:57:20
01:23:01:02
projected
in the secret cinema of my head.

	•
	01:23:02:14
	01:23:05:10
Я отвечал Петру на его вопрос.	A minha resposta era ao Piotr.
	•
	01:23:06:06
	01:23:09:18
Мы - два кинематографиста, разговорившиеся в ночи.	Éramos dois cineastas a falar às tantas da noite.
	•
	01:23:11:08
	01:23:13:16
Я разыгрывал роль перед Петром.	Eu estava a representar para o Piotr.
	•
	01:23:14:02
	01:23:16:20
Я знал, что он,	Dei-lhe algo que sabia que ele compreenderia
	•
	01:23:16:22
	01:23:18:20
как кинорежиссёр, поймёт меня.	enquanto homem de cinema.
	•
	01:23:19:00
	01:23:20:14
Но я сказал Петру,	Mas disse ao Piotr

•
01:23:02:14
01:23:05:10
C'est à Piotr que j'ai répondu.

•
01:23:02:14
01:23:05:10
My answer was to Piotr.

•
01:23:06:06
01:23:09:18
Nous étions deux cinéastes en train de discuter tard dans la nuit.

•
01:23:06:10
01:23:09:18
We were two filmmakers
talking late at night.

•
01:23:11:08
01:23:13:16
Je jouais pour Piotr.

•
01:23:11:08
01:23:13:16
I was performing to Piotr.

•
01:23:14:06
01:23:18:00
Je lui donnais quelque chose
qu'il comprendrait en tant que cinéaste.

•
01:23:14:06
01:23:18:00
I gave him something I knew
he would understand as a filmmaker.

•
01:23:19:00
01:23:20:14
Mais j'ai dit à Piotr

•
01:23:19:00
01:23:20:14
But I told Piotr

	• 01:23:20:16 01:23:22:16
что я помню многое,	que me lembrava de muitas coisas
	• 01:23:22:18 01:23:24:02
чего никогда не было.	que nunca tinham acontecido.
	• 01:23:24:16 01:23:27:04
Никогда не случалось со мной.	Que nunca me tinham acontecido.
	• 01:23:28:00 01:23:33:06
Многое, что я помню, но в то же время знаю, что я это «снял»,	Coisas de que me lembro mas que sei ter «filmado»
	• 01:23:33:12 01:23:35:12
чтобы не забыть.	para poder lembrar-me delas.
	• 01:23:36:16 01:23:39:08
Я помню мужчину, который рылся в карманах,	Lembro-me de um homem a remexer nos bolsos,

•
01:23:20:16
01:23:22:16
que je me souvenais
de beaucoup de choses

•
01:23:20:16
01:23:22:00
that I remembered many things

•
01:23:22:18
01:23:24:02
qui n'étaient jamais arrivées.

•
01:23:22:02
01:23:23:18
that had never happened.

•
01:23:24:16
01:23:27:04
Qui ne m'étaient jamais arrivées.

•
01:23:24:16
01:23:27:04
That never happened to me.

•
01:23:28:00
01:23:33:06
Des choses dont je me rappelais
mais que j'avais «filmées»

•
01:23:28:00
01:23:33:06
Things that I remember
but that I know I "filmed"

•
01:23:33:12
01:23:35:12
pour pouvoir m'en souvenir.

•
01:23:33:12
01:23:35:12
so that I could remember them.

•
01:23:36:16
01:23:39:08
Je me souviens d'un homme
fouillant dans ses poches,

•
01:23:36:16
01:23:39:08
I remember a man
going through his pockets,

	• 01:23:39:18 01:23:42:12
всё что-то искал, снова и снова,	à procura de qualquer coisa, repetidamente,
	• 01:23:42:18 01:23:43:22
стыдясь	com ar de envergonhado
	• 01:23:43:24 01:23:46:12
своего пустого, неуместного беспокойства.	da trivialidade da sua preocupação tão despropositada.
	• 01:23:47:02 01:23:48:22
В двубортном костюме.	Com um fato de trespasse.
	• 01:23:49:18 01:23:51:24
В нем не было ничего особенного.	Um homem sem nada de especial.
	• 01:23:53:08 01:23:55:08
Я не знаю, кто он такой,	Não sei quem era,

•

01:23:39:18
01:23:42:12
à la recherche de quelque chose
qu'il ne trouvait pas,

•

01:23:39:18
01:23:42:12
searching for something
over and over,

•

01:23:42:18
01:23:46:12
l'air honteux de son inquiétude futile,
déplacée.

•

01:23:42:18
01:23:46:12
looking ashamed of his trivial,
out-of-place worry.

•

01:23:47:02
01:23:48:22
Dans un costume croisé.

•

01:23:47:02
01:23:48:22
In a double-breasted suit.

•

01:23:49:18
01:23:51:24
Rien chez lui
n'attirait l'attention.

•

01:23:49:18
01:23:51:24
Nothing remarkable about him.

•

01:23:53:08
01:23:55:08
Je ne sais pas qui il était,

•

01:23:53:08
01:23:57:16
I don't know who he was, nor why
he was at my father's funeral,

•

01:23:55:10
01:23:57:16

и почему он на похоронах
моего отца,

nem por que estava
no funeral do meu pai,

•

01:23:58:08
01:24:00:24

хотя на самом деле его там не было

apesar de nunca lá ter estado.

•

01:24:02:11
01:24:04:20

Свет, падающий
на его тёмный костюм,

A luz a cair sobre
o seu fato escuro,

•

01:24:05:08
01:24:08:20

его отворачивающееся лицо
в дверном проёме.

a cara virada para o outro lado,
debaixo da ombreira de uma porta.

•

01:24:09:16
01:24:12:04

Я могу снять его руки
крупным планом,

Posso fazer um grande plano
das mãos.

•

01:24:12:06
01:24:13:16

что я и делаю.

E faço-o.

•

01:23:55:10
01:23:57:16
ni pourquoi il assistait
à l'enterrement de mon père,

•

01:23:58:08
01:24:00:24
même s'il n'a jamais été là.

•

01:23:58:08
01:24:00:24
even though he was never there.

•

01:24:02:11
01:24:04:20
La lumière sur son costume
sombre,

•

01:24:02:11
01:24:04:20
The light on his dark suit,

•

01:24:05:08
01:24:08:20
son visage tourné vers l'extérieur
dans l'encadrement de la porte.

•

01:24:05:08
01:24:08:20
his face turned away
under a door frame.

•

01:24:09:16
01:24:12:04
Je peux faire un gros plan
sur ses mains.

•

01:24:09:16
01:24:13:12
I can zoom in on the hands.
And I do.

•

01:24:12:06
01:24:13:16
Et je le fais.

•
01:24:14:22
01:24:16:18

Что я также помню,	Que me lembro também

•
01:24:16:20
01:24:18:20

как я ходил по городам,	de andar por cidades

•
01:24:19:06
01:24:21:02

в которых я никогда не был.	onde nunca estive.

•
01:24:21:10
01:24:23:10

По уродливым бетонным городам	Cidades feias, de cimento,

•
01:24:23:12
01:24:26:22

и городам, где у каждого дома был сад.	e cidades onde cada casa tem um jardim.

•
01:24:27:16
01:24:29:14

Звуки трамваев и сирен,	O som de eléctricos e sirenes

•

01:24:14:22
01:24:16:18
Je lui ai dit que
je me souvenais aussi

•

01:24:14:23
01:24:18:00
That I remembered also
walking through cities

•

01:24:16:20
01:24:18:20
d'avoir marché dans des villes

•

01:24:19:06
01:24:21:02
where I have never been.

•

01:24:19:06
01:24:21:02
que je n'ai jamais visitées.

•

01:24:21:10
01:24:23:10
Des villes de béton, hideuses,

•

01:24:21:10
01:24:23:10
Ugly, concrete cities

•

01:24:23:12
01:24:26:22
et des villes dans lesquelles
chaque maison a un jardin.

•

01:24:23:12
01:24:26:22
and cities where every house
has a garden.

•

01:24:27:16
01:24:29:14
Du bruit des trams et des sirènes

•

01:24:27:16
01:24:32:10
The sound of trams and sirens
that are not the ones I have heard.

	• 01:24:30:10 01:24:32:18
но не те, что я слышал.	que não são as que alguma vez ouvi.
	• 01:24:33:10 01:24:35:18
Женщина в двери магазина,	Uma mulher à porta da sua loja,
	• 01:24:37:18 01:24:40:14
разговаривающая с мужчиной через дорогу.	a falar com um homem do outro lado da rua.
	• 01:24:41:02 01:24:42:22
Их слова пересекают дорогу, полную	As suas palavras atravessando o trânsito
	• 01:24:43:00 01:24:44:16
легковых машин,	de carros,
	• 01:24:44:18 01:24:45:24
грузовиков,	camiões,

•

01:24:30:10
01:24:32:18
qui ne sont pas ceux que j'ai entendus.

•

01:24:33:10
01:24:35:18
Une femme à la porte
de sa boutique,

•

01:24:37:18
01:24:40:14
discutant avec un homme
de l'autre côté de la rue.

•

01:24:41:02
01:24:42:22
Leurs paroles traversant le flot

•

01:24:43:00
01:24:44:16
des voitures,

•

01:24:44:18
01:24:45:24
des camions,

•

01:24:33:10
01:24:35:18
A woman at her shop's door,

•

01:24:37:18
01:24:40:14
talking to a man across the street.

•

01:24:41:02
01:24:42:22
Their words crossing the traffic

•

01:24:43:00
01:24:44:16
of cars,

•

01:24:44:18
01:24:45:24
lorries,

	• 01:24:46:02 01:24:47:10
автобусов.	autocarros.
	• 01:24:47:20 01:24:51:00
Они изо всех сил стараются расслышать друг друга.	Fazem um esforço para se entenderem.
	• 01:24:51:20 01:24:53:22
Как называется этот город?	Que nome tem esta cidade?
	• 01:24:57:18 01:25:00:06
Мои родители родились в Москве.	Tanto o meu pai como a minha mãe nasceram em Moscovo.
	• 01:25:00:14 01:25:03:02
Я родился в Сибири, в Иркутске.	Eu nasci na Sibéria, em Irkutsk.
	• 01:25:03:14 01:25:06:00
Мой отец был инженером- строителем.	O meu pai era engenheiro civil.

•
01:24:46:02
01:24:47:10
des autobus.

•
01:24:46:02
01:24:47:10
buses.

•
01:24:47:20
01:24:51:00
Ils ont du mal
à se comprendre.

•
01:24:47:20
01:24:51:00
They struggle to understand
each other.

•
01:24:51:20
01:24:53:22
Comment s'appelle cette ville ?

•
01:24:51:20
01:24:53:22
What's this city's name?

•
01:24:57:18
01:25:00:06
Mes parents
sont nés à Moscou.

•
01:24:57:18
01:25:00:06
Both my parents
were born in Moscow.

•
01:25:00:14
01:25:03:02
Je suis né en Sibérie,
à Irkoutske.

•
01:25:00:14
01:25:03:02
I was born in Siberia,
in Irkutsk.

•
01:25:03:14
01:25:06:00
Mon père était ingénieur
du génie civil.

•
01:25:03:14
01:25:06:00
My father was a structural engineer.

•

01:25:06:08
01:25:07:18

Его послали в Иркутск

Tinham-no mandado para Irkutsk
para trabalhar

•

01:25:07:20
01:25:10:24

строить электростанцию
на Ангаре.

na grande central hidroeléctrica
em construção no rio Angara.

•

01:25:11:10
01:25:14:00

Моя мама была
учительницей музыки.

A minha mãe
era professora de música.

•

01:25:15:02
01:25:18:00

Они поженились сразу
после того, как она окончила

Casaram-se assim que ela terminou

•

01:25:18:02
01:25:20:18

Московскую консерваторию.

os seus estudos no
Conservatório de Moscovo.

•

01:25:21:10
01:25:23:08

Несколько месяцев спустя

Poucos meses depois,

•
01:25:06:08
01:25:07:18
Il avait été envoyé à Irkoutske
pour travailler

•
01:25:06:08
01:25:07:18
He had been sent to Irkutsk

•
01:25:07:20
01:25:10:24
dans la centrale hydro-électrique
en construction sur l'Angara.

•
01:25:07:20
01:25:10:24
to work on the big hydro-electric plant
being constructed on the Angara.

•
01:25:11:10
01:25:14:00
Ma mère enseignait la musique.

•
01:25:11:10
01:25:14:00
My mother was a music teacher.

•
01:25:15:02
01:25:18:00
Elle venait de terminer ses études
au conservatoire de Moscou

•
01:25:15:02
01:25:18:00
She had just finished her studies
at the Moscow Conservatoire

•
01:25:18:02
01:25:20:18
lorsqu'ils se sont mariés.

•
01:25:18:02
01:25:20:18
when they married.

•
01:25:21:10
01:25:23:08
Quelques mois plus tard

•
01:25:21:10
01:25:23:08
A few months later

	• 01:25:23:10 01:25:25:00
они переехали в Сибирь.	mudaram-se para a Sibéria.
	• 01:25:29:08 01:25:32:10
В детстве у меня не было сада или парка.	Em criança não tive nem um jardim nem um parque.
	• 01:25:33:00 01:25:34:20
У меня был Байкал.	Tive o Lago Baikal.
	• 01:25:35:04 01:25:35:20
Огромный	O imenso,
	• 01:25:35:22 01:25:36:22
и прекрасный,	maravilhoso
	• 01:25:37:14 01:25:39:09
таинственный Байкал.	e misterioso Baikal.

•

01:25:23:10
01:25:25:00
ils sont partis pour la Sibérie.

•

01:25:23:10
01:25:25:00
they moved to Siberia.

•

01:25:29:08
01:25:32:02
Enfant,
je n'avais ni parc ni jardin.

•

01:25:29:08
01:25:32:02
As a child I didn't have a garden,
or a park.

•

01:25:33:00
01:25:34:20
J'avais le lac Baïkal.

•

01:25:33:00
01:25:34:20
I had the Lake Baikal.

•

01:25:35:04
01:25:35:20
L'immense,

•

01:25:35:04
01:25:35:20
The immense,

•

01:25:35:22
01:25:36:22
le magnifique,

•

01:25:35:22
01:25:36:22
and beautiful,

•

01:25:37:14
01:25:39:09
le mystérieux Baïkal.

•

01:25:37:14
01:25:39:09
mysterious Baikal.

•

01:25:40:18
01:25:42:16

Я с нетерпением ждал воскресений,	Esperava impacientemente pelos domingos,

•

01:25:42:18
01:25:45:08

чтобы поехать на Байкал с отцом.	para ir até lá de carro com o meu pai.

•

01:25:47:00
01:25:49:02

Мы редко ездили туда зимой,	No Inverno era raro lá irmos,

•

01:25:49:04
01:25:54:16

но бывали там почти каждое воскресенье поздней весной и летом.	mas íamos quase todos os domingos no fim da Primavera e no Verão.

•

01:25:55:14
01:25:57:16

У моего отца там был друг,	O meu pai tinha lá um amigo,

•

01:25:57:18
01:26:00:08

доктор, который работал в санатории.	um médico do sanatório.

•
01:25:40:18
01:25:42:16
J'attendais les dimanches
avec impatience

•
01:25:42:18
01:25:45:08
pour m'y rendre en voiture
avec mon père.

•
01:25:47:00
01:25:49:02
Nous n'y allions pas souvent
l'hiver,

•
01:25:49:04
01:25:54:16
mais presque tous les dimanches
à la fin du printemps et en été.

•
01:25:55:14
01:25:57:16
Mon père avait un ami là-bas,

•
01:25:57:18
01:26:00:08
un médecin qui travaillait
dans le sanatorium.

•
01:25:40:20
01:25:42:12
I waited impatiently
for Sundays

•
01:25:42:14
01:25:45:08
to drive there with my father.

•
01:25:47:00
01:25:49:02
We didn't often go in winter,

•
01:25:49:04
01:25:54:16
but almost every Sunday
in late spring and summer.

•
01:25:55:14
01:25:57:16
My father had a friend there,

•
01:25:57:18
01:26:00:08
a doctor at the sanatorium.

•

01:26:01:06
01:26:03:02

Я не помню, как его звали,
Não consigo lembrar-me
do seu nome,

•

01:26:03:14
01:26:05:18

но несколько лет назад
mas reconheci-o há uns anos

•

01:26:05:20
01:26:07:20

я узнал его в чеховском
Иване Нюхине,
em Ivan Niúkhin,

•

01:26:08:16
01:26:10:08

когда прочёл впервые
quando li pela primeira vez

•

01:26:10:10
01:26:12:08

«О вреде табака».
«Os malefícios do tabaco»,
de Tchékhov.

•

01:26:12:18
01:26:14:20

Он был невысокий и худой,
Era baixo e magro,

•

01:26:01:06
01:26:03:02
Je ne me rappelle pas de son nom,

•

01:26:01:06
01:26:03:02
I can't remember his name,

•

01:26:03:14
01:26:05:18
mais je l'ai reconnu
en Ivan Nyoukhine

•

01:26:03:14
01:26:08:08
but I recognized him in Ivan Nyukhin
some years ago

•

01:26:05:20
01:26:07:20
quand j'ai lu pour la première fois,

•

01:26:08:16
01:26:10:08
il y a quelques années,

•

01:26:08:10
01:26:10:08
when I read for the first time

•

01:26:10:10
01:26:12:08
«Les maléfices du tabac»
de Tchékhov.

•

01:26:10:10
01:26:12:04
Chekhov's "Smoking is bad for you".

•

01:26:12:18
01:26:14:20
Il était petit et mince

•

01:26:12:18
01:26:14:20
He was short and thin

	• 01:26:14:22 01:26:16:10
с густыми бакенбардами	com patilhas espessas
	• 01:26:16:12 01:26:18:12
и редеющими волосами.	e o cabelo ralo.
	• 01:26:19:20 01:26:23:00
Его жена работала старшей сестрой в санатории.	A sua mulher era emfermeira-chefe no sanatório.
	• 01:26:24:08 01:26:26:16
У неё был устрашающий вид.	Tinha um ar de meter medo.
	• 01:26:27:06 01:26:30:14
Крупная женщина с очень чёрными волосами,	Uma mulher enorme com um cabelo muito escuro,
	• 01:26:30:16 01:26:32:08
густыми бровями	sobrancelhas carregadas,

•

01:26:14:22
01:26:16:10
avec des pattes broussailleuses

•

01:26:14:22
01:26:16:10
with bushy sideburns

•

01:26:16:12
01:26:18:12
et il perdait ses cheveux.

•

01:26:16:12
01:26:18:12
and thinning hair.

•

01:26:19:20
01:26:23:00
Sa femme était infirmière en chef
au sanatorium.

•

01:26:19:20
01:26:23:00
His wife was a senior nurse
at the sanatorium.

•

01:26:24:08
01:26:26:16
Elle avait un air terrifiant.

•

01:26:24:08
01:26:26:16
She looked terrifying.

•

01:26:27:06
01:26:30:14
C'était une femme imposante
avec des cheveux très noirs,

•

01:26:27:06
01:26:30:14
A big woman
with very black hair,

•

01:26:30:16
01:26:31:20
d'épais sourcils,

•

01:26:30:16
01:26:31:20
heavy eyebrows,

•

01:26:32:10
01:26:36:08

и таким выражением лица,
как будто её вот-вот вырвет.

e a expressão
de alguém prestes a vomitar.

•

01:26:37:02
01:26:41:14

Я много раз слышал,
как он жаловался на её
отвратительный характер.

Surprendi-o muitas vezes
a queixar-se da sua mesquinhez.

•

01:26:42:06
01:26:43:16

Доктор...

O médico...

•

01:26:44:02
01:26:46:06

Жаль, что я не помню его имени.

Não consigo
lembrar-me do nome dele,

•

01:26:47:16
01:26:49:22

Но думаю, что когда-
нибудь вспомню...

mas logo me ocorrerá...

•

01:26:51:06
01:26:52:12

У доктора была дочь,

O médico tinha uma filha,

•

•

01:26:31:22
01:26:36:08
et l'air de quelqu'un
sur le point de vomir.

•

01:26:37:02
01:26:41:14
Je l'ai surpris bien des fois se plaignant
de son manque de cœur.

•

01:26:42:06
01:26:43:16
Le docteur...

•

01:26:44:02
01:26:46:06
J'aimerais me souvenir de son nom,

•

01:26:47:16
01:26:49:22
mais ça me reviendra...

•

01:26:51:06
01:26:52:12
Le docteur avait une fille,

•

01:26:31:22
01:26:36:08
and the expression of someone
who was about to throw-up.

•

01:26:37:02
01:26:41:14
I overheard him many times
complaining about her meanness.

•

01:26:42:06
01:26:43:16
The doctor...

•

01:26:44:02
01:26:46:06
I wish I could remember his name,

•

01:26:47:16
01:26:49:22
but it will come back to me...

•

01:26:51:06
01:26:52:12
The doctor had a daughter,

	• 01:26:52:14 01:26:53:18
Ольга.	a Olga.
	• 01:26:53:20 01:26:57:00
Ольга была на 2 или 3 года старше меня.	A Olga era 2 ou 3 anos mais velha do que eu.
	• 01:26:57:16 01:27:00:08
У неё были густые брови, как у матери,	Tinha as mesmas sobrancelhas grossas da sua mãe,
	• 01:27:00:10 01:27:02:10
сросшиеся на переносице.	unidas a meio.
	• 01:27:03:04 01:27:04:10
Но она была красавицей,	Mas era linda,
	• 01:27:04:14 01:27:06:10
с большими грустными глазами	com uns olhos enormes, tristes,

•

01:26:52:14
01:26:53:18
Olga.

•

01:26:52:14
01:26:53:18
Olga.

•

01:26:53:20
01:26:57:00
Olga était de 2 ou 3 ans mon aînée.

•

01:26:53:20
01:26:57:00
Olga was 2 or 3 years older than me.

•

01:26:57:16
01:27:00:08
Elle avait les sourcils épais
de sa mère,

•

01:26:57:16
01:27:00:08
She had the thick eyebrows
of her mother,

•

01:27:00:10
01:27:02:10
qui se rejoignaient au milieu.

•

01:27:00:10
01:27:02:10
joining in the middle.

•

01:27:03:04
01:27:04:10
Mais elle était belle,

•

01:27:03:04
01:27:04:10
But she was beautiful,

•

01:27:04:14
01:27:06:10
avec ses grands yeux tristes,

•

01:27:04:12
01:27:06:10
with big, sad eyes,

•

01:27:06:12
01:27:08:20

и замечательной
застенчивой улыбкой.

e um sorriso tímido, encantador.

•

01:27:09:22
01:27:12:10

Она была моей первой любовью.

Foi o meu primeiro amor.

•

01:27:17:18
01:27:19:04

Я любил Байкал,

Eu adorava o Baikal,

•

01:27:19:06
01:27:23:04

потому что для меня Ольга
и Байкал сливались в одно целое.

porque o Baikal
e a Olga eram um só.

•

01:27:23:16
01:27:26:08

Меня укачивало

Embora os solavancos
dos buracos na estrada

•

01:27:26:10
01:27:28:08

в дороге
от тряски по выбоинам,

me fizessem enjoar
no carro,

•

01:27:06:12
01:27:08:20
et un sourire timide, charmant.

•

01:27:06:12
01:27:08:20
and a lovely, shy smile.

•

01:27:09:22
01:27:12:10
Elle a été mon premier amour.

•

01:27:09:22
01:27:12:10
She was my first love.

•

01:27:17:18
01:27:19:04
J'aimais le Baïkal

•

01:27:17:18
01:27:19:04
I loved the Baikal

•

01:27:19:06
01:27:23:04
parce qu'Olga et lui
ne faisaient qu'un.

•

01:27:19:06
01:27:23:04
because Olga and the Baikal
were one.

•

01:27:23:16
01:27:26:18
Même si les trous sur la route
qui secouaient la voiture

•

01:27:24:04
01:27:26:00
Even if all the bumping
over the potholes in the road

•

01:27:26:20
01:27:28:08
me rendaient malade,

•

01:27:26:02
01:27:27:02
made me sick,

	• 01:27:28:10 01:27:30:08
но я страстно мечтал о встрече с ней.	eu só queria lá estar com ela.
	• 01:27:30:14 01:27:31:14
Гулять с ней	A andar com ela,
	• 01:27:31:16 01:27:34:14
впереди или позади наших отцов.	à frente ou atrás dos nossos pais.
	• 01:27:34:16 01:27:36:10
Летом собирать малину,	No Verão, a apanhar framboesas,
	• 01:27:36:12 01:27:38:00
красную и чёрную смородину	groselhas vermelhas e pretas,

•

01:27:28:10
01:27:30:08
mon seul désir était
d'être là-bas auprès d'elle.

•

01:27:27:04
01:27:29:20
I longed to be there with her.

•

01:27:30:14
01:27:31:14
De marcher à ses côtés,

•

01:27:30:16
01:27:31:14
Walking with her

•

01:27:31:16
01:27:34:14
devant ou derrière nos pères.

•

01:27:31:16
01:27:34:06
ahead of or behind our fathers.

•

01:27:34:16
01:27:36:20
L'été,
nous ramassions des framboises,

•

01:27:34:16
01:27:35:14
In summer,

•

01:27:36:22
01:27:38:00
des groseilles, du cassis,

•

01:27:35:16
01:27:36:20
picking raspberries,

•

01:27:36:22
01:27:38:00
red and black currants,

•

01:27:38:02
01:27:40:00

и жимолость.

e madressilva.

•

01:27:40:08
01:27:43:06

У неё всегда был с собой
маленький
носовой платочек,

Ela levava sempre um lencinho,

•

01:27:43:12
01:27:45:18

чтобы вытирать рот
и руки.

para limpar a boca
e as mãos.

•

01:27:47:16
01:27:50:00

Если по дороге
нам попадался ручей,

Se passávamos por um riacho

•

01:27:50:14
01:27:52:20

она мочила платочек в воде,

ela molhava-o,

•

01:27:52:22
01:27:55:00

выкручивала его
и била о камень,

torcia-o
e batia-o contra uma pedra,

•

01:27:38:02
01:27:40:00
et du chèvrefeuille.

•

01:27:38:02
01:27:40:00
and honeysuckle.

•

01:27:40:08
01:27:43:06
Elle portait toujours
un petit mouchoir,

•

01:27:40:08
01:27:43:06
She always carried a small
handkerchief,

•

01:27:43:12
01:27:45:18
pour s'essuyer la bouche
et les mains.

•

01:27:43:12
01:27:45:18
to wipe her mouth
and her hands.

•

01:27:47:16
01:27:50:00
Lorsque nous traversions
un ruisseau,

•

01:27:47:16
01:27:50:00
If we crossed a stream,

•

01:27:50:14
01:27:53:10
elle le trempait dans l'eau,

•

01:27:50:14
01:27:53:10
she would dip it in water,

•

01:27:53:12
01:27:55:00
l'essorait et le frappait
contre une pierre,

•

01:27:53:12
01:27:55:00
wring it and flap it against a stone,

•

01:27:55:02
01:27:58:08

а потом вытирала пальцы,
один за другим,

e limpava os dedos
um por um,

•

01:27:58:10
01:27:59:02

медленно,

lentamente,

•

01:27:59:04
01:28:00:02

нежно,

delicadamente,

•

01:28:00:10
01:28:03:12

как врачи и сиделки
протирают раны.

como os médicos e as enfermeiras
limpam as feridas.

•

01:28:04:00
01:28:06:12

Зимой и весной
мы играли в снегу,

No Inverno e na Primavera
brincávamos com a neve,

•
01:27:55:02
01:27:56:20
and wipe her fingers

•
01:27:55:02
01:27:58:08
et s'essuyait les doigts
un à un,

•
01:27:56:22
01:27:58:08
one by one,

•
01:27:58:10
01:27:59:02
lentement,

•
01:27:58:10
01:27:59:02
slowly,

•
01:27:59:04
01:28:00:02
avec douceur,

•
01:27:59:04
01:28:00:02
gently,

•
01:28:00:10
01:28:03:12
comme les docteurs et les infirmières
lorsqu'ils nettoyent les plaies.

•
01:28:00:10
01:28:03:12
as doctors and nurses wipe wounds.

•
01:28:04:00
01:28:06:12
En hiver et au printemps
nous jouions avec la neige,

•
01:28:04:00
01:28:05:02
In winter and spring

•

01:28:06:14
01:28:09:16

бурили палками лёд,

fazíamos buracos
na neve com paus,

•

01:28:09:18
01:28:12:16

и она то и дело
стряхивала снег с тёплых варежек,

e ela batia constantemente
as luvas grossas

•

01:28:12:18
01:28:14:20

похлопывая одну о другую.

para as limpar da neve.

•
01:28:06:14
01:28:09:16
nous faisions des trous dans la glace
avec des bâtons,

•
01:28:09:18
01:28:12:16
et elle tapotait
encore et encore ses gants épais

•
01:28:12:18
01:28:14:20
pour se débarrasser de la neige.

•
01:28:05:04
01:28:07:00
we would play with the snow,

•
01:28:07:02
01:28:08:20
bore holes in the ice with sticks,

•
01:28:08:22
01:28:10:08
and she would again

•
01:28:10:10
01:28:11:02
and again

•
01:28:11:04
01:28:13:08
pat her thick gloves together

•
01:28:13:10
01:28:14:12
to get rid of the snow.

•

01:28:19:14
01:28:20:24

В начале этого века,

No princípio deste século,

•

01:28:21:02
01:28:24:20

когда вода замерзала и паромы не
могли плавать,

quando os barcos
ficavam presos no gelo,

•

01:28:24:22
01:28:26:24

путешественники, укутанные
в тулупы,

os viajantes eram envoltos
em peles de carneiro,

•

01:28:27:02
01:28:28:12

грузили огромные корзины

metidos
nuns cestos enormes

•

01:28:28:14
01:28:30:16

на санные упряжки

em trenós
puxados a cavalos

•

01:28:30:20
01:28:33:02

и перебирались
через Байкал.

e levados até
a outra margem do Baikal.

•
01:28:19:14
01:28:22:14
Au début de ce siècle,

•
01:28:22:18
01:28:24:20
lorsque les transbordeurs
étaient pris dans les glaces,

•
01:28:24:24
01:28:26:24
les voyageurs étaient enveloppés
de peaux de mouton,

•
01:28:27:02
01:28:28:12
placés dans d'énormes paniers

•
01:28:28:14
01:28:30:16
sur des traîneaux tirés
par des chevaux,

•
01:28:30:20
01:28:33:02
et conduits de l'autre côté.

•
01:28:19:14
01:28:22:14
At the beginning of this century,

•
01:28:22:18
01:28:24:14
when the ferries became ice-bound,

•
01:28:24:24
01:28:26:24
travellers would be wrapped
in sheepskins,

•
01:28:27:02
01:28:28:12
put in huge baskets

•
01:28:28:14
01:28:30:16
on the back of horse sleighs

•
01:28:30:20
01:28:33:02
and ferried across.

	• 01:28:34:00 01:28:36:02
Кажется, 2000 санных упряжек	Parece que mais de 2000 trenós
	• 01:28:36:04 01:28:39:16
одновременно пересекали Байкал туда и обратно	cruzavam o Baikal ao mesmo tempo,
	• 01:28:39:18 01:28:42:08
со скоростью 10 километров в час.	à velocidade de 10 km à hora.
	• 01:28:43:06 01:28:45:06
Я читал об этом в книгах,	Isto foi o que li nos livros,
	• 01:28:45:14 01:28:48:14
а сам я видел, как большие тёмные грузовики	mas o que vi foram camiões, enormes e escuros,
	• 01:28:48:16 01:28:50:14
и мотоциклы с коляской	e motocicletas com carros laterais,

•

01:28:34:00
01:28:36:02
Il paraît qu'à une certaine époque,

•

01:28:34:00
01:28:36:02
It seems that over 2000 sleighs

•

01:28:36:04
01:28:39:16
plus de 2000 traîneaux faisaient
l'aller-retour sur le Baïkal

•

01:28:36:04
01:28:39:16
criss-crossed the Baikal at one time,

•

01:28:39:18
01:28:42:08
à une vitesse de 10 km/heure.

•

01:28:39:18
01:28:42:08
at a speed of 10 km an hour.

•

01:28:43:06
01:28:45:06
Ça, je l'ai lu dans des livres,

•

01:28:43:06
01:28:45:06
This I read in books,

•

01:28:45:14
01:28:48:14
mais je n'ai vu
que d'énormes camions sombres,

•

01:28:45:14
01:28:48:14
but what I saw were large,
dark lorries,

•

01:28:48:16
01:28:50:14
et des motos
avec des side-cars,

•

01:28:48:16
01:28:50:14
and motorbikes with sidecars,

	• 01:28:50:16 01:28:52:18
пересекали замёрзший Байкал	a atravessar as águas geladas,
	• 01:28:52:20 01:28:54:12
бесшумно вдалеке.	silenciosamente, ao longe.
	• 01:28:55:20 01:28:58:12
Иной мир, спрятанный подо льдом в три метра толщиной,	Escondido por baixo de 3 metros de gelo,
	• 01:28:58:16 01:29:01:02
продолжал свою жизнь.	um outro mundo continuava a viver.
	• 01:29:01:10 01:29:04:12
А нам, чтобы снова увидеть его,	E teríamos de esperar pelo fim de Junho
	• 01:29:04:14 01:29:05:22
приходилось ждать до конца июня.	para voltar a vê-lo.

•
01:28:50:16
01:28:52:18
traversant les eaux gelées,

•
01:28:52:20
01:28:54:12
silencieusement, au loin.

•
01:28:55:20
01:28:58:12
Caché sous 3 mètres de glace,

•
01:28:58:16
01:29:01:02
un autre monde continuait à vivre.

•
01:29:01:10
01:29:04:12
Et nous devions attendre
la fin du mois de juin

•
01:29:04:14
01:29:05:22
pour le revoir.

•
01:28:50:16
01:28:52:18
driving across the frozen waters,

•
01:28:52:20
01:28:54:12
silently, far away.

•
01:28:55:20
01:28:58:12
Hidden below 3 metres of ice,

•
01:28:58:16
01:29:01:02
another world continued to live.

•
01:29:01:10
01:29:03:12
And we would have to wait
until the end of June

•
01:29:03:14
01:29:05:18
to see it again.

	• 01:29:06:12 01:29:09:06
Мне нравилось читать и слушать военные истории	Eu gostava de ler e ouvir histórias de manobras militares
	• 01:29:09:08 01:29:11:14
о том, как армии	de quando o exército usava o Baikal
	• 01:29:11:16 01:29:13:18
перебрасывали подкрепления через Байкал.	para enviar reforços de emergência.
	• 01:29:14:06
Как князь Хилков	01:29:18:02
решил проложить железную дорогу по льду	Como quando o Príncipe Khilkov decidiu assentar carris sobre o gelo,
	• 01:29:18:06 01:29:20:16
от Порта Байкал до Танхоя.	entre o Porto Baikal e Tankhoi.
	• 01:29:21:04 01:29:22:18
Японцы атаковали,	Os japoneses tinham atacado,

•

01:29:06:12
01:29:09:06
J'aimais lire et écouter
des histoires de militaires,

•

01:29:09:08
01:29:11:14
lorsque le Baïkal
était utilisé par l'armée

•

01:29:11:16
01:29:13:18
pour envoyer d'urgence
des renforts sur l'autre rive.

•

01:29:14:06
01:29:18:02
Comme lorsque le Prince Khilkov
décida de poser des rails sur la glace,

•

01:29:18:06
01:29:20:16
entre le port Baïkal et Tankhoï.

•

01:29:21:04
01:29:22:18
Les japonais avaient attaqué

•

01:29:06:12
01:29:09:06
I liked reading and hearing stories
of the military,

•

01:29:09:08
01:29:11:14
of when the Baikal
was used by the army

•

01:29:11:16
01:29:13:18
to rush reinforcements across it.

•

01:29:14:06
01:29:18:02
Like when Prince Khilkov
decided to run rails across the ice,

•

01:29:18:06
01:29:20:16
from Port Baikal to Tankhoi.

•

01:29:21:04
01:29:22:18
The Japanese had attacked

	• 01:29:22:20 01:29:25:02
и он хотел переправить русские войска	e ele queria fazer com que as tropas russas
	• 01:29:25:04 01:29:26:08
как можно быстрее.	atravessassem depressa.
	• 01:29:26:16 01:29:28:06
Чтобы испытать новую дорогу,	Como teste,
	• 01:29:28:08 01:29:31:00
он пустил по льду поезд.	enviou primeiro uma locomotiva.
	• 01:29:31:04 01:29:32:08
Был февраль,	Era Fevereiro,
	• 01:29:32:10 01:29:34:00
но тёплые источники	mas as nascentes quentes

•

01:29:22:20
01:29:24:14
et il voulait faire traverser
les troupes russes

•

01:29:22:20
01:29:26:04
and he wanted to get
Russian troops across, fast.

•

01:29:24:16
01:29:26:08
le plus rapidement possible.

•

01:29:26:16
01:29:28:06
Il fit une tentative

•

01:29:26:18
01:29:31:00
He sent in a test locomotive.

•

01:29:28:08
01:29:31:00
avec une locomotive.

•

01:29:31:04
01:29:32:08
C'était en février,

•

01:29:31:04
01:29:32:08
It was February,

•

01:29:32:10
01:29:34:00
mais des sources d'eau chaude

•

01:29:32:10
01:29:36:04
but warm springs
had started to melt the ice.

	• 01:29:34:02 01:29:36:04
подогревали лёд, и он начал таять.	tinham começado a derreter o gelo.
	• 01:29:36:16 01:29:38:16
Поезд летел сотни метров,	O comboio mergulhou centenas de metros
	• 01:29:38:18 01:29:42:00
пока не достиг дна,	pelas águas até ao fundo do lago,
	• 01:29:42:02 01:29:44:20
оставив во льду пролом в 20 километров длиной.	deixando uma brecha no gelo de mais de 20 km de comprimento.
	• 01:29:45:20 01:29:47:16
Я смотрел на замёрзший Байкал,	Eu olhava para o Baikal gelado,
	• 01:29:47:18 01:29:48:24
тихий и огромный,	tranquilo e gigantesco,

•
01:29:34:02
01:29:36:04
commençaient déjà
à faire fondre la glace.

•
01:29:36:16
01:29:40:00
Le train fit un plongeon
de plusieurs centaines de mètres

•
01:29:36:16
01:29:38:12
The train plunged
hundreds of metres

•
01:29:40:02
01:29:42:00
jusqu'au fond du lac,

•
01:29:38:22
01:29:42:12
through the water
to the lake bed,

•
01:29:42:02
01:29:44:20
déchirant la glace
sur une longueur de plus de 20 km.

•
01:29:42:14
01:29:44:18
leaving a gash in the ice
of over 20 km in length.

•
01:29:45:20
01:29:47:16
Je regardais le Baïkal gelé,

•
01:29:45:20
01:29:47:20
I would look at the frozen Baikal,

•
01:29:47:18
01:29:48:24
immobile et gigantesque,

•
01:29:47:22
01:29:48:16
still and gigantic,

	•
	01:29:49:02 01:29:51:00
и закрывал глаза.	e fechava os olhos.
	•
	01:29:52:00 01:29:55:20
Я пытался представить двадцатикилометровый пролом.	Tentava imaginar essa fractura de 20 km.
	•
	01:29:56:12 01:29:57:18
И не мог.	E não conseguia.
	•
	01:29:58:06 01:29:59:22
Мои глаза открывались,	Os meus olhos voltavam a abrir-se
	•
	01:29:59:24 01:30:02:00
прежде чем я мог представить его.	antes de conseguir vê-la.
	•
	01:30:03:16 01:30:07:16
20 километров - это слишком много, чтобы представить.	20 km eram longos demais para conseguir imaginá-los.

•
01:29:49:02
01:29:51:00
et je fermais les yeux.

•
01:29:48:18
01:29:50:20
and I would close my eyes.

•
01:29:52:00
01:29:55:20
J'essayais d'imaginer
la brèche de 20 km.

•
01:29:52:00
01:29:55:20
I would try to imagine
the 20 km long crack.

•
01:29:56:12
01:29:57:18
Mais je n'y arrivais pas.

•
01:29:56:12
01:29:57:18
And I couldn't.

•
01:29:58:06
01:29:59:22
Mes yeux se rouvraient

•
01:29:58:06
01:29:59:22
My eyes would open again

•
01:29:59:24
01:30:02:00
avant que je puisse la voir.

•
01:29:59:24
01:30:02:00
before I could see it.

•
01:30:03:16
01:30:07:16
20 km, c'était trop long
pour l'imaginer.

•
01:30:03:16
01:30:07:16
20 km was too long to imagine.

	• 01:30:08:18 01:30:11:10
Байкалу 25 миллионов лет,	O Baikal tinha 25 milhões de anos,
	• 01:30:11:12 01:30:14:00
и я тоже не мог это представить.	e isso também eu não conseguia imaginar.
	• 01:30:14:16 01:30:16:08
25 миллионов.	25 milhões.
	• 01:30:16:20 01:30:17:18
Мне было девять	Eu tinha 9
	• 01:30:17:20 01:30:19:04
или десять лет.	ou 10 anos.
	• 01:30:20:12 01:30:22:00
Мне тогда казалось странным,	Nessa altura fazia-me confusão

•

01:30:08:18
01:30:11:10
Le Baïkal avait
25 millions d'années,

•

01:30:08:18
01:30:11:10
The Baikal was 25 million years old,

•

01:30:11:12
01:30:14:00
et ça non plus
je ne pouvais pas l'imaginer.

•

01:30:11:12
01:30:14:00
and I couldn't imagine that either.

•

01:30:14:16
01:30:16:08
25 millions.

•

01:30:14:16
01:30:16:08
25 million.

•

01:30:16:20
01:30:17:18
J'en avais 9,

•

01:30:16:20
01:30:17:18
I was 9,

•

01:30:17:20
01:30:19:04
ou 10.

•

01:30:17:20
01:30:19:04
or 10.

•

01:30:20:12
01:30:22:00
A l'époque, j'étais perplexe

•

01:30:20:12
01:30:22:00
It puzzled me then

	• 01:30:22:02 01:30:24:08
что о трагедии князя Хилкова	que a história do desastre do Príncipe Khilkov
	• 01:30:24:10 01:30:26:06
рассказывали по-разному.	fosse contada também doutra maneira.
	• 01:30:26:08 01:30:28:20
Кое-кто говорил, что поезд затонул	Havia quem dissesse que a locomotiva se afundou
	• 01:30:28:22 01:30:30:02
в неглубоком месте,	num baixio do Baikal,
	• 01:30:30:04 01:30:32:06
что его спасли,	que tinha sido recuperada,
	• 01:30:32:08 01:30:34:18
и после этого он много лет ходил	e que depois tinha servido muitos anos

•

01:30:22:02
01:30:24:08
à l'idée que l'on puisse
raconter d'une autre façon

•

01:30:24:10
01:30:26:06
l'histoire du désastre
du Prince Khilkov.

•

01:30:26:08
01:30:28:18
Certains disaient
que la locomotive était tombée

•

01:30:28:20
01:30:32:00
dans une partie peu profonde
du Baïkal,

•

01:30:32:02
01:30:34:00
qu'elle fut récupérée
et remise en service

•

01:30:34:02
01:30:37:02
pendant de nombreuses années
entre St Pétersbourg et Helsinki.

•

01:30:22:02
01:30:24:08
that the story
of Prince Khilkov's disaster

•

01:30:24:10
01:30:26:06
was also told in a different way.

•

01:30:26:08
01:30:27:10
Some said

•

01:30:27:12
01:30:29:20
that the locomotive sunk
in a shallow part of the Baikal,

•

01:30:29:22
01:30:32:00
that it was salvaged,

•

01:30:32.02
01:30:34:00
and that it ran
for many years after

	• 01:30:34:20 01:30:37:20
между Санкт-Петербургом и Хельсинки.	na linha entre S. Petersburgo e Helsínquia.
	• 01:30:41:02 01:30:43:02
И я спросил отца	Então perguntei ao meu pai
	• 01:30:46:04 01:30:48:04
какой же истории верить.	qual delas era a história verdadeira.
	• 01:30:49:06 01:30:53:04
Отец сказал, что история с трагичным концом правдива.	O meu pai disse que a história do desastre era a verdadeira.
	• 01:30:54:18 01:30:57:06
Глубина Байкала 1 километр,	O Baikal tem mais de 1 km de profundidade.
	• 01:30:58:10 01:31:01:06
Полтора в самом глубоком месте.	Um e meio na parte mais funda.

•
01:30:34:02
01:30:36:16
between St Petersburg and Helsinki.

•
01:30:41:02
01:30:43:02
Alors j'ai demandé à mon père

•
01:30:41:02
01:30:43:02
So I asked my father

•
01:30:46:04
01:30:48:04
laquelle de ces histoires était vraie.

•
01:30:46:04
01:30:48:04
which one was the true story.

•
01:30:49:06
01:30:53:04
Il m'a répondu que celle
du désastre était la vraie.

•
01:30:49:06
01:30:53:04
My father said the disaster story
was the true one.

•
01:30:54:18
01:30:57:06
Le Baïkal a une profondeur
d'un kilomètre,

•
01:30:54:18
01:30:57:06
The Baikal is over 1 km deep,

•
01:30:58:10
01:31:01:06
un kilomètre et demi
au plus profond.

•
01:30:58:10
01:31:01:06
one and a half at its deepest.

•

01:31:02:14
01:31:06:04

Никаких шансов на спасение
у поезда не было.

Não havia hipótese alguma de terem
conseguido salvar a locomotiva.

•

01:31:08:08
01:31:10:06

Потом я спросил учительницу,

E perguntei
à minha professora,

•

01:31:10:08
01:31:13:10

и она сказала, что история со
счастливым концом,

e ela disse que a história
que acabava bem

•

01:31:13:12
01:31:15:18

возможно, правдива.

era provavelmente
a verdadeira.

•

01:31:17:14
01:31:20:06

Люди не стали бы зря говорить,
что поезд

Não iriam inventar
que a locomotiva

•

01:31:20:08
01:31:25:00

регулярно ходит
между такими большими городами,

fizera regularmente o trajecto
entre duas cidades tão grandes

•

01:31:02:14
01:31:06:04
Il était impossible qu'ils aient pu
récupérer cette locomotive.

•

01:31:08:08
01:31:10:06
J'ai aussi demandé
à ma professeur,

•

01:31:10:08
01:31:13:10
qui m'a dit que l'histoire
qui se terminait bien

•

01:31:13:12
01:31:15:18
était probablement vraie.

•

01:31:17:14
01:31:20:06
On n'aurait pas inventé
que la locomotive

•

01:31:20:08
01:31:25:00
ait effectué des trajets réguliers
entre des villes aussi importantes

•

01:31:02:14
01:31:06:04
There was no chance they could
have salvaged that locomotive.

•

01:31:08:08
01:31:10:06
And I asked my teacher,

•

01:31:10:08
01:31:13:10
and she said
that the happy-ending one

•

01:31:13:12
01:31:15:18
was probably the true story.

•

01:31:17:14
01:31:20:06
They wouldn't have invented
that the locomotive

•

01:31:20:08
01:31:25:00
had made regular trips
between such big towns

	• 01:31:25:08 01:31:27:12
если бы это было неправдой.	se isso não fosse verdade.
	• 01:31:29:18 01:31:31:14
Потом я спросил маму,	E perguntei à minha mãe,
	• 01:31:31:16 01:31:33:14
и она сказала, что иногда	e ela disse-me que às vezes
	• 01:31:33:16 01:31:37:02
все эти истории - выдумка.	não há verdade alguma nestas histórias.
	• 01:31:37:16 01:31:39:22
Потому что время проходит,	Porque com o andar do tempo
	• 01:31:40:20 01:31:42:06
люди забывают	as pessoas esquecem-se

•

01:31:25:08
01:31:27:12
si ce n'était pas vrai.

•

01:31:25:08
01:31:27:12
if it weren't true.

•

01:31:29:18
01:31:31:14
Alors,
j'ai demandé à ma mère,

•

01:31:29:18
01:31:31:14
And I asked my mother,

•

01:31:31:16
01:31:33:14
et elle m'a répondu
que parfois

•

01:31:31:16
01:31:33:14
and she said that sometimes

•

01:31:33:16
01:31:37:02
il n'y a rien de vrai
dans ce genre d'histoire.

•

01:31:33:16
01:31:37:02
there is no truth to these stories.

•

01:31:37:16
01:31:39:22
Parce qu'avec le temps

•

01:31:37:16
01:31:39:22
Because as time passes

•

01:31:40:20
01:31:42:06
les gens oublient

•

01:31:40:20
01:31:42:06
people forget

	• 01:31:42:14 01:31:44:06
и путаются.	e fazem confusões.
	• 01:31:48:18 01:31:53:02
Я был разочарован во всех ответах, которые получил.	Fiquei desiludido com todas as respostas que me deram.
	• 01:31:54:04 01:31:55:24
Но в ответе моего отца	Mas a do meu pai
	• 01:31:56:08 01:31:58:19
смысла было больше, чем в других.	era a que fazia mais sentido.
	• 01:31:59:18 01:32:03:02
Я доверял ему, когда дело касалось знаний.	No que dizia respeito a saber coisas, eu confiava nele.
	• 01:32:07:14 01:32:09:22
В Москве, до переезда в Иркутск	Ainda em Moscovo, antes da mudança para Irkutsk,

•
01:31:42:14
01:31:44:06
et ne savent plus très bien.

•
01:31:42:14
01:31:44:06
and become confused.

•
01:31:48:18
01:31:53:24
Moi, j'étais déçu
par toutes ces réponses.

•
01:31:48:18
01:31:53:24
For my part I was disappointed
with all of the answers I got.

•
01:31:54:04
01:31:55:24
Mais celle de mon père

•
01:31:54:04
01:31:55:24
But my father's

•
01:31:56:08
01:31:58:19
semblait la plus logique.

•
01:31:56:08
01:31:58:19
made the most sense.

•
01:31:59:18
01:32:02:20
Je lui faisais confiance
pour ces choses-là.

•
01:31:59:18
01:32:02:20
I trusted him when it came
to knowing things.

•
01:32:07:14
01:32:09:22
A Moscou,
avant de déménager à Irkoutske,

•
01:32:07:14
01:32:09:22
Back in Moscow,
before the move to Irkutsk,

•

01:32:10:06
01:32:12:20

мой отец вступил в партию.	o meu pai tinha entrado para o Partido.

•

01:32:13:16
01:32:15:12

Мама вступила позднее,	A minha mãe entrou depois,

•

01:32:16:00
01:32:19:24

и то, только для того, чтобы доставить отцу удовольствие.	e só para lhe fazer a vontade.

•

01:32:21:10
01:32:22:12

Однажды вечером,	Uma noite,

•

01:32:22:14
01:32:25:10

много лет спустя после смерти отца,	muitos anos depois da morte do meu pai,

•
01:32:10:06
01:32:12:20
mon père avait rejoint le Parti.

•
01:32:10:06
01:32:12:20
my father had joined the Party.

•
01:32:13:16
01:32:15:12
Ma mère l'a fait plus tard,

•
01:32:13:16
01:32:15:12
My mother joined later,

•
01:32:16:00
01:32:17:08
mais uniquement

•
01:32:16:00
01:32:17:08
and then

•
01:32:17:10
01:32:19:24
pour lui faire plaisir.

•
01:32:17:10
01:32:19:24
only to please him.

•
01:32:21:10
01:32:22:12
Un soir,

•
01:32:21:10
01:32:22:12
One evening,

•
01:32:22:14
01:32:25:10
bien après la mort de mon père,

•
01:32:22:14
01:32:25:10
many years after my father's death,

•

01:32:26:00
01:32:28:02

она рассказала мне, как ненавидела

ela disse-me
como tinha detestado

•

01:32:28:04
01:32:30:02

партийные собрания,

as reuniões do Partido,

•

01:32:31:02
01:32:34:20

бесконечные выступления
и духоту комнат.

os discursos intermináveis
e o ar abafado das salas.

•

01:32:35:08
01:32:37:12

Её спасала музыка.

A música viera salvá-la.

•

01:32:37:18
01:32:39:10

За день до собрания

Na véspera de cada reunião,

•

01:32:39:22
01:32:43:04

она ходила в школьную библиотеку,
выбирала ноты,

ela ia à biblioteca da escola,
escolhia uma partitura,

•
01:32:26:00
01:32:28:02
elle m'a avoué combien
elle avait détesté

•
01:32:26:00
01:32:29:20
she told me how much she had hated
Party meetings,

•
01:32:28:04
01:32:30:02
les réunions du Parti,

•
01:32:31:02
01:32:34:20
les discours interminables et
l'odeur de renfermé dans les pièces.

•
01:32:31:02
01:32:34:20
the interminable speeches
and the stale air in the rooms.

•
01:32:35:08
01:32:37:12
La musique était venue la sauver.

•
01:32:35:08
01:32:37:12
Music came to her rescue.

•
01:32:37:18
01:32:39:10
La veille des réunions

•
01:32:37:18
01:32:39:10
The day before one
of those meetings

•
01:32:39:22
01:32:43:04
elle se rendait à la bibliothèque
de l'école et prenait une partition,

•
01:32:39:22
01:32:43:04
she would go to the school library
and pick a score,

запоминала их	• 01:32:43:22 01:32:45:14 estudava-a,
и потом, на собрании	• 01:32:46:00 01:32:47:16 e depois, durante a reunião,
наигрывала музыку про себя.	• 01:32:47:22 01:32:50:02 tocava-a na cabeça.
Окруженная музыкой, она была неуязвима.	• 01:32:52:00 01:32:55:12 Sentia-se segura dentro da sua música.
Она рассказывала об этом с улыбкой.	• 01:33:01:00 01:33:03:14 Disse-mo com o sorriso
Так улыбаются только старики,	• 01:33:04:10 01:33:06:04 que só os velhos têm,

•

01:32:43:22
01:32:45:14
l'étudiait,

•

01:32:43:22
01:32:45:14
study it,

•

01:32:46:00
01:32:47:16
puis, pendant la réunion,

•

01:32:46:00
01:32:47:16
and then, at the meeting,

•

01:32:47:22
01:32:50:02
elle la jouait dans sa tête.

•

01:32:47:22
01:32:50:02
she would be playing it in her head.

•

01:32:52:00
01:32:55:12
Elle se sentait à l'abri
dans sa musique.

•

01:32:52:00
01:32:55:12
She was safe inside her music.

•

01:33:01:00
01:33:03:14
Elle m'a dit cela avec le sourire

•

01:33:01:00
01:33:03:14
She said it with the smile

•

01:33:04:10
01:33:06:04
que seuls ont les gens âgés

•

01:33:04:10
01:33:06:04
that only old people have

	• 01:33:06:06 01:33:08:08
когда говорят о чём-то,	quando falam de alguma coisa
	• 01:33:08:10 01:33:11:06
что случилось много лет назад.	que aconteceu há muito tempo.
	• 01:33:12:18 01:33:14:22
Улыбка - это расстояние	Esse sorriso é a distância
	• 01:33:14:24 01:33:16:18
между настоящим	entre o tempo presente
	• 01:33:16:20 01:33:20:04
и временем, когда то событие произошло.	e o tempo de quando isso aconteceu.
	• 01:33:21:20 01:33:23:00
Когда я был маленьким,	Em criança

•

01:33:06:06
01:33:08:08
lorsqu'ils parlent
de quelque chose

•

01:33:06:06
01:33:08:08
when they talk of something

•

01:33:08:10
01:33:11:06
qui s'est produit
il y a longtemps.

•

01:33:08:10
01:33:11:06
that happened long ago.

•

01:33:13:00
01:33:15:04
Ce sourire, c'est la distance

•

01:33:13:00
01:33:15:04
That smile is the distance

•

01:33:15:06
01:33:16:18
entre le moment présent

•

01:33:15:06
01:33:16:18
between the time now

•

01:33:16:20
01:33:20:04
et celui où ce
«quelque chose» a eu lieu.

•

01:33:16:20
01:33:20:04
and the time when it happened.

•

01:33:21:20
01:33:23:00
Quand j'étais enfant,

•

01:33:21:20
01:33:23:00
As a child

•

01:33:23:02
01:33:24:14

я слышал истории,

ouvia
como se fossem histórias

•

01:33:24:16
01:33:27:12

которые взрослые обсуждали друг
с другом.

as conversas
dos adultos entre eles.

•

01:33:28:08
01:33:31:00

Часто это были даже не истории,

Muitas vezes
não eram bem histórias,

•

01:33:31:02
01:33:34:08

а просто самые обыкновенные
разговоры.

apenas as conversas
mais triviais.

•

01:33:35:10
01:33:37:00

Но то, что они рассказывали,

Mas o que quer que dissessem

•

01:33:37:02
01:33:38:24

поражало меня так же,

tinha o mesmo poder

•

01:33:23:02
01:33:24:14
je prenais pour des histoires

•

01:33:23:02
01:33:24:14
I overheard as stories

•

01:33:24:16
01:33:27:12
les conversations
des adultes entre eux.

•

01:33:24:16
01:33:27:12
the conversations of adults
between themselves.

•

01:33:28:08
01:33:31:00
Souvent, il ne s'agissait pas
de véritables histoires,

•

01:33:28:08
01:33:31:00
They were often not proper stories,

•

01:33:31:02
01:33:34:08
tout simplement d'un échange
de propos insignifiants.

•

01:33:31:02
01:33:34:08
just the most trivial of exchanges.

•

01:33:35:10
01:33:37:00
Mais ce qu'ils disaient

•

01:33:35:10
01:33:37:00
But whatever they said

•

01:33:37:02
01:33:38:24
avait le même pouvoir
que les légendes

•

01:33:37:02
01:33:38:24
had the same power as captions

•

01:33:39:06
01:33:42:04

как подписи под картинками
в книгах.

que as legendas
por baixo das ilustrações nos livros.

•

01:33:43:02
01:33:46:20

Этого было достаточно,
чтобы заставить меня задуматься.

O bastante para eu fantasiar.

•

01:33:48:10
01:33:51:00

Лучшие истории были в книгах,

As melhores histórias
vinham nos livros,

•

01:33:51:08
01:33:54:08

а их было много у моего отца.

e o meu pai tinha muitos.

•

01:34:00:12
01:34:03:00

Князь Хилков был моим героем.

O Príncipe Khilkov
era um dos meus heróis.

•

01:34:04:08
01:34:06:16

И дело не в трагедии с поездом,

Não por causa
do desastre da locomotiva,

•
01:33:39:06
01:33:42:04
sous les illustrations dans les livres.

•
01:33:39:06
01:33:42:04
under the illustrations in books.

•
01:33:43:02
01:33:46:20
Cela suffisait à me rendre songeur.

•
01:33:43:02
01:33:46:20
Enough to make me wonder.

•
01:33:48:10
01:33:51:00
Les meilleures histoires
étaient dans les livres,

•
01:33:48:10
01:33:51:00
The best stories were in books,

•
01:33:51:08
01:33:54:08
et mon père en avait beaucoup.

•
01:33:51:08
01:33:54:08
and my father had many.

•
01:34:00:12
01:34:03:00
Le Prince Khilkov était
l'un de mes héros.

•
01:34:00:12
01:34:03:00
Prince Khilkov was a hero of mine.

•
01:34:04:08
01:34:06:16
Pas à cause
du désastre de la locomotive,

•
01:34:04:08
01:34:06:16
Not because
of the locomotive disaster,

	• 01:34:07:04 01:34:09:10
а потому что я прочитал в книжке,	mas porque tinha lido num livro
	• 01:34:09:16 01:34:12:12
что в молодости он уехал в Америку	que ele tinha ido para a América quando ainda era rapaz,
	• 01:34:12:14 01:34:16:08
и работал там инкогнито на железных дорогах,	e trabalhado incógnito nos caminhos-de-ferro americanos
	• 01:34:16:18 01:34:18:18
чтобы узнать о них побольше.	para assim poder estudá-los.
	• 01:34:19:16 01:34:21:10
Мне нравилось это слово:	Como eu gostava dessa palavra:
	• 01:34:21:12 01:34:23:04
инкогнито.	incógnito.

•
01:34:07:04
01:34:09:10
mais parce que j'avais lu
dans un livre

•
01:34:07:04
01:34:09:10
but because I had read in a book

•
01:34:09:16
01:34:12:12
que lorsqu'il était jeune,
il était allé en Amérique

•
01:34:09:16
01:34:12:12
that he had gone to America
as a young man

•
01:34:12:14
01:34:16:08
et avait travaillé incognito
pour les chemins de fer

•
01:34:12:14
01:34:16:08
and worked incognito
for the American railways,

•
01:34:16:18
01:34:18:12
afin de pouvoir les étudier.

•
01:34:16:18
01:34:18:12
so that he could study them.

•
01:34:19:16
01:34:21:10
Comme j'aimais ce mot :

•
01:34:19:16
01:34:21:10
I loved that word:

•
01:34:21:12
01:34:23:04
incognito.

•
01:34:21:12
01:34:23:04
incognito.

•

01:34:23:16
01:34:26:13
Мне казалось, | Viver incógnito

•

01:34:26:21
01:34:28:20
что самая замечательная жизнь - | era para mim a mais nobre

•

01:34:29:12
01:34:31:24
это жизнь инкогнито. | das formas de vida.

•

01:34:32:19
01:34:34:22
Беглецы и революционеры живут инкогнито. | Vive-se incógnito

•

01:34:35:16
01:34:37:08
se se é um fugitivo,

•

01:34:37:10
01:34:38:12
ou um revolucionário.

•

01:34:23:16
01:34:26:13
Garder l'incognito

•

01:34:26:21
01:34:28:20
était pour moi la plus noble

•

01:34:29:12
01:34:31:24
façon de vivre.

•

01:34:32:19
01:34:34:22
On vit dans l'incognito

•

01:34:35:16
01:34:37:08
lorsqu'on est un fugitif,

•

01:34:37:10
01:34:38:12
ou un révolutionnaire.

•

01:34:23:16
01:34:26:13
To be incognito

•

01:34:26:21
01:34:28:20
was to me the noblest

•

01:34:29:12
01:34:31:24
of ways to live.

•

01:34:32:19
01:34:34:22
You live incognito

•

01:34:35:16
01:34:37:08
if you are a fugitive,

•

01:34:37:10
01:34:38:12
or a revolutionary.

	• 01:34:39:04 01:34:42:08
Скрываются, чтобы их не нашли.	Tem-se cuidado para não se ser descoberto.
	• 01:34:42:10 01:34:44:06
Но жить инкогнито можно также,	Mas pode-se também viver incógnito
	• 01:34:44:08 01:34:46:16
если вы выполняете важнейшую миссию.	se a nossa missão é da mais alta ordem.
	• 01:34:51:08 01:34:53:18
Жил-был жестокий старик по имени Байкал.	Um tirano conhecido como Starik Baikal
	• 01:34:53:20 01:34:55:04 ou Velho Baikal
	• 01:34:56:04 01:34:57:22
Жил он в озере,	vivia no lago

•

01:34:39:04
01:34:42:08
On prend des précautions
pour ne pas être découvert.

•

01:34:42:10
01:34:44:06
Mais on peut
aussi garder l'incognito

•

01:34:44:08
01:34:46:16
lorsque la mission qu'on remplit
est de la plus haute importance.

•

01:34:51:08
01:34:53:20
Un tyran appelé Starik Baïkal,

•

01:34:53:22
01:34:55:00
ou Baïkal l'Ancien,

•

01:34:56:04
01:34:57:22
vivait dans le lac,

•

01:34:39:04
01:34:42:08
You take precautions
not to be discovered.

•

01:34:42:10
01:34:44:06
But you can be incognito also

•

01:34:44:08
01:34:46:16
if your mission is
of the highest order.

•

01:34:51:08
01:34:53:20
A tyrant known as Starik Baikal,

•

01:34:53:22
01:34:55:00
or Old Baikal,

•

01:34:56:04
01:34:57:22
lived in the lake

•

01:34:59:00
01:35:02:16

и было у него 336 сыновей	com os seus 336 filhos

•

01:35:02:24
01:35:04:08

и одна дочь,	e com sua única filha:

•

01:35:04:10
01:35:06:06

красавица Ангара.	a bela Angara.

•

01:35:07:12
01:35:10:06

Его сыновья верно служили ему,	Os filhos serviam-no fielmente

•

01:35:10:14
01:35:12:08

наполняя озеро водой.	trazendo-lhe a água,

•

01:35:13:12
01:35:15:14

А Ангара была в заточении	mas Angara estava prisioneira

•
01:34:59:00
01:35:02:16
avec ses 336 fils

•
01:34:59:00
01:35:02:16
with 336 sons

•
01:35:02:24
01:35:04:08
et son unique fille :

•
01:35:02:24
01:35:04:08
and his only daughter:

•
01:35:04:10
01:35:06:06
la belle Angara.

•
01:35:04:10
01:35:06:06
the beautiful Angara.

•
01:35:07:12
01:35:10:06
Ses fils le servaient fidèlement,

•
01:35:07:12
01:35:10:06
His sons faithfully poured
in the water,

•
01:35:10:14
01:35:12:08
lui ramenant de l'eau

•
01:35:13:12
01:35:15:10
mais Angara était prisonnière

•
01:35:10:14
01:35:12:08
but Angara was imprisoned

	• 01:35:16:04 01:35:18:08
за то, что отказалась выйти замуж	porque se recusava a casar
	• 01:35:18:10 01:35:20:12
за Иркут-реку.	com o rio Irkut.
	• 01:35:22:00 01:35:24:02
Птицы, прилетавшие с севера,	As aves aquáticas do Norte
	• 01:35:24:08 01:35:26:18
рассказывали ей о Енисее,	trouxeram-lhe novas de Ienissei,
	• 01:35:26:20 01:35:28:12
красавце-богатыре,	um formoso gigante,
	• 01:35:29:12 01:35:31:12
и она полюбила молодца,	e ela acabou por se apaixonar

•
01:35:16:04
01:35:18:08
car elle refusait d'épouser

•
01:35:13:12
01:35:15:10
because she refused to marry

•
01:35:18:10
01:35:20:12
le fleuve Irkout.

•
01:35:16:04
01:35:20:09
the Irkut river.

•
01:35:22:00
01:35:24:02
Des oiseaux aquatiques
venant du nord

•
01:35:22:00
01:35:24:02
Water birds from the North

•
01:35:24:08
01:35:26:18
lui apportaient
des nouvelles de Ienissei,

•
01:35:24:08
01:35:26:18
brought her news of Yenisei,

•
01:35:26:20
01:35:28:12
un beau géant,

•
01:35:26:20
01:35:28:12
a handsome giant,

•
01:35:29:12
01:35:31:12
et avec le temps,
elle tomba amoureuse

•
01:35:29:12
01:35:31:12
and in time she fell in love

•

01:35:31:18
01:35:34:06

хотя никогда не встречала его.

por este herói que nunca vira.

•

01:35:35:08
01:35:37:08

Однажды ненастной ночью

Numa noite de tempestade

•

01:35:37:10
01:35:39:22

Ангара вырвалась из заточения

Angara conseguiu libertar-se

•

01:35:40:00
01:35:42:02

и убежала к Енисею.

para se unir a Ienissei.

•

01:35:43:06
01:35:48:04

Её отец проснулся,
но было слишком поздно
отправляться в погоню.

O pai acordou tarde demais
para poder impedi-la,

•

01:35:49:06
01:35:52:08

Он метнул валун вслед,

mas lançou-lhe um pedregulho.

•
01:35:31:18
01:35:34:06
de ce héros
qu'elle n'avait jamais vu.

•
01:35:31:18
01:35:34:06
with this hero she had never seen.

•
01:35:35:08
01:35:37:08
Par une nuit d'orage

•
01:35:35:08
01:35:37:08
One stormy night

•
01:35:37:10
01:35:39:22
Angara s'enfuit de sa prison

•
01:35:37:10
01:35:39:22
Angara broke out of her prison

•
01:35:40:00
01:35:42:02
pour s'unir à Ienissei.

•
01:35:40:00
01:35:42:02
to be united with Yenisei.

•
01:35:43:06
01:35:48:04
Son père se réveilla
trop tard pour l'arrêter,

•
01:35:43:06
01:35:48:04
Her father woke up
too late to stop her,

•
01:35:49:06
01:35:52:08
mais lui lança un énorme rocher.

•
01:35:49:06
01:35:52:08
but hurled a boulder after her.

	• 01:35:53:12 01:35:55:08
но промахнулся.	Não a atingiu,
	• 01:35:55:10 01:35:58:06
И стоит тот валун по сей день посреди реки Ангары.	e ainda hoje está no meio do rio Angara.
	• 01:36:03:14 01:36:05:06
Это - сказание о реках,	Esta é uma história de rios,
	• 01:36:05:08 01:36:07:18
одно из многих, сложенных бурятским народом	uma das muitas histórias da gente da Buriátia,
	• 01:36:07:20 01:36:10:00
на далёких берегах.	na margem de lá,

•

01:35:53:12
01:35:54:12
Il la manqua,

•

01:35:54:14
01:35:56:12
et le rocher se trouve maintenant

•

01:35:56:14
01:35:58:06
au milieu de la rivière Angara.

•

01:36:03:14
01:36:05:06
Cette histoire,
c'est une histoire de rivières,

•

01:36:05:08
01:36:07:18
l'une des nombreuses histoires
du peuple bouryat,

•

01:36:07:20
01:36:10:00
sur l'autre rive,

•

01:35:53:12
01:35:54:12
It missed,

•

01:35:54:14
01:35:56:12
and now stands mid-stream

•

01:35:56:14
01:35:58:06
in the Angara river.

•

01:36:03:14
01:36:05:06
This is a story of rivers,

•

01:36:05:08
01:36:07:18
one of the many stories
of the Buryat people,

•

01:36:07:20
01:36:10:00
on the far shore,

Шаманы передают эти сказания из поколения в поколение.	• 01:36:11:20 01:36:15:18 contada pelos xamãs de geração em geração.
Как-то вечером,	• 01:36:21:08 01:36:22:06 Uma noite,
когда я уже засыпал в своей комнате,	• 01:36:22:08 01:36:24:22 estava já eu na cama,
я услышал, как отец рассказывал маме	• 01:36:25:08 01:36:29:16 ouvi do quarto o meu pai a contar à minha mãe
историю, случившуюся на самом деле.	• 01:36:29:18 01:36:30:24 uma história verdadeira.
Он слышал её от итальянца,	• 01:36:32:08 01:36:34:16 Tinha-lhe sido contada por um italiano

•
01:36:11:20
01:36:15:18
racontée par les shamans
de génération en génération.

•
01:36:11:20
01:36:15:18
told by shamans from
generation to generation.

•
01:36:21:08
01:36:22:06
Une nuit,

•
01:36:21:08
01:36:22:06
One night,

•
01:36:22:08
01:36:24:22
déjà bordé dans mon lit,

•
01:36:22:08
01:36:24:22
already tucked up in bed,

•
01:36:25:08
01:36:29:16
j'ai entendu mon père
qui racontait à ma mère

•
01:36:25:08
01:36:29:16
I overheard from my room
my father telling my mother

•
01:36:29:18
01:36:30:24
une histoire vraie.

•
01:36:29:18
01:36:30:24
a true story.

•
01:36:32:08
01:36:34:16
Il la tenait d'un italien

•
01:36:32:08
01:36:34:16
It had been told to him
by an Italian man

	• 01:36:34:18 01:36:37:04
члена итальянской компартии,	membro do Partido Comunista Italiano,
	• 01:36:38:06 01:36:39:04
инженера, как и отец,	também ele engenheiro,
	• 01:36:39:06 01:36:42:02
приехавшего в Иркутск.	que tinha vindo visitar Irkutsk.
	• 01:36:43:12 01:36:46:18
Речь шла о двух стариках, муже и жене,	Era a história de um casal de velhos
	• 01:36:46:22 01:36:49:00
его соседях в Риме.	que vivia ao lado da sua casa em Roma.
	• 01:36:49:12 01:36:51:18
Я представлял себе Рим	Eu imaginava Roma como uma cidade muito escura,

•
01:36:34:18
01:36:37:04
membre du parti communiste italien,

•
01:36:34:18
01:36:37:04
from the Italian Communist Party,

•
01:36:38:06
01:36:39:04
ingénieur lui aussi,

•
01:36:38:06
01:36:39:04
also an engineer,

•
01:36:39:06
01:36:42:02
en visite à Irkoutske.

•
01:36:39:06
01:36:42:02
who had come to visit Irkutsk.

•
01:36:43:12
01:36:46:18
C'était l'histoire
d'un vieux couple

•
01:36:43:12
01:36:46:18
This was the story
of an old couple

•
01:36:46:22
01:36:49:00
qui vivait à côté de chez lui,
à Rome.

•
01:36:46:22
01:36:49:00
who lived next to his house in Rome.

•
01:36:49:12
01:36:51:18
Je m'imaginais Rome comme
une ville très sombre,

•
01:36:49:12
01:36:53:02
I thought of Rome as a very dark
city, far, far away,

•

01:36:51:20
01:36:53:10

как далёкий сумрачный город,

muito, muito distante,

•

01:36:53:12
01:36:56:01

где жил Папа Римский,

onde vivia o Papa

•

01:36:56:04
01:36:58:16

и куда я никогда не попаду.

e onde eu nunca iria.

•

01:36:59:22
01:37:03:08

Старики эти проработали
на почте всю жизнь,

Este casal de velhos tinha trabalhado
toda a vida para os correios

•

01:37:03:20
01:37:05:22

пока не вышли на пенсию.

e estavam agora reformados.

•

01:37:07:10
01:37:09:14

Их нельзя было назвать
неприветливыми,

Não era que fossem antipáticos,

•

01:36:51:20
01:36:53:04
lointaine, très, très lointaine,

•

01:36:53:06
01:36:56:01
où vivait le Pape

•

01:36:53:06
01:36:56:01
where the Pope lived

•

01:36:56:04
01:36:58:16
et où je n'irais jamais.

•

01:36:56:04
01:36:58:16
and I would never go.

•

01:36:59:22
01:37:03:08
Ces gens avaient travaillé
toute leur vie pour la Poste

•

01:36:59:22
01:37:03:08
These old people had worked all their
lives for the Post Office,

•

01:37:03:20
01:37:05:22
et étaient à la retraite.

•

01:37:03:20
01:37:05:22
and they were now retired.

•

01:37:07:10
01:37:09:14
Ils n'étaient pas antipathiques,

•

01:37:07:10
01:37:09:14
They were not unfriendly,

	• 01:37:10:16 01:37:14:04
но они вели замкнутый образ жизни.	mas eram de poucas falas.
	• 01:37:15:10 01:37:18:02
Соседи видели, как они всё время	Durante meses os vizinhos tinham-nos visto
	• 01:37:18:10 01:37:20:08
выходили из своей квартиры и опять возвращались,	a entrar e a sair a qualquer hora,
	• 01:37:20:12 01:37:22:08
таская большие	carregando sempre
	• 01:37:23:00 01:37:24:18
чёрные	com grandes sacos pretos
	• 01:37:24:20 01:37:27:12
полиэтиленовые мешки.	de plástico.

•

01:37:10:16
01:37:14:04
mais restaient très discrets.

•

01:37:10:16
01:37:14:04
but kept to themselves.

•

01:37:15:10
01:37:18:02
Pendant des mois,
les voisins les avaient vus

•

01:37:15:10
01:37:18:02
For months the neighbours
had seen them

•

01:37:18:10
01:37:20:08
aller et venir à toute heure,

•

01:37:18:10
01:37:20:08
coming and going at all hours,

•

01:37:20:12
01:37:22:08
portant de grands sacs

•

01:37:20:12
01:37:22:08
always carrying big,

•

01:37:23:00
01:37:24:18
noirs

•

01:37:23:00
01:37:24:18
black,

•

01:37:24:20
01:37:27:12
en plastique.

•

01:37:24:20
01:37:27:12
plastic bags.

	• 01:37:29:00 01:37:32:02
В доме появился отвратительный запах.	Começou então a pairar um cheiro péssimo no prédio.
	• 01:37:33:02 01:37:35:16
Его все почувствовали.	Toda a gente o sentia.
	• 01:37:37:02 01:37:40:06
Выяснилось, что запах исходит с верхнего этажа,	Descobriram que vinha do andar de cima,
	• 01:37:41:14 01:37:43:20
где жили эти старики.	onde vivia o casal de velhos.
	• 01:37:44:22 01:37:46:12
К ним стучались,	Tocavam à campainha,
	• 01:37:46:14 01:37:48:12
но они не отвечали.	mas eles não respondiam.

•
01:37:29:00
01:37:32:02
Puis une horrible puanteur
a commencé à envahir le bâtiment.

•
01:37:29:00
01:37:32:02
Then, an awful smell
began lingering in the building.

•
01:37:33:02
01:37:35:16
Tout le monde pouvait la sentir.

•
01:37:33:02
01:37:35:16
Everyone could smell it.

•
01:37:37:02
01:37:40:06
Les voisins se sont aperçus
qu'elle arrivait du dernier étage,

•
01:37:37:02
01:37:40:06
They traced it to the top floor,

•
01:37:41:14
01:37:43:20
où vivait le vieux couple.

•
01:37:41:14
01:37:43:20
where the old couple lived.

•
01:37:44:22
01:37:46:12
Ils sonnaient à la porte,

•
01:37:44:22
01:37:46:12
They rang the bell,

•
01:37:46:14
01:37:48:12
mais les vieux
ne répondaient jamais.

•
01:37:46:14
01:37:48:12
but they wouldn't answer.

	• 01:37:49:02 01:37:52:06
Когда соседи встречали их на лестнице	Quando os viam nas escadas,
	• 01:37:52:14 01:37:54:12
и жаловались на запах,	falavam-lhes no cheiro.
	• 01:37:54:20 01:37:58:18
старики говорили, что они ничего не замечают.	Os velhos diziam que não tinham dado por nada.
	• 01:38:00:02 01:38:02:16
И так продолжалось месяцами.	E assim continuou durante meses.
	• 01:38:03:22 01:38:06:00
На лестнице завелись мыши,	Apareceram ratos na escada.
	• 01:38:06:20 01:38:08:18
а потом крысы.	E depois, ratazanas.

•

01:37:49:02
01:37:52:06
Lorsqu'ils les voyaient
dans les escaliers

•

01:37:49:02
01:37:52:06
When they saw them in the stairs

•

01:37:52:14
01:37:54:12
ils leur parlaient
de cette odeur.

•

01:37:52:14
01:37:54:12
they would tell them about the smell.

•

01:37:54:20
01:37:58:18
Ils répondaient qu'ils n'avaient
rien remarqué.

•

01:37:54:20
01:37:58:18
The old couple would say they
hadn't noticed.

•

01:38:00:02
01:38:02:16
Et cela a continué
pendant des mois.

•

01:38:00:02
01:38:02:16
And so it went on for months.

•

01:38:03:22
01:38:06:00
Des souris sont apparues
dans les escaliers,

•

01:38:03:22
01:38:06:00
Mice appeared on the stairs,

•

01:38:06:20
01:38:08:18
puis des rats.

•

01:38:06:20
01:38:08:18
and then rats.

	•
	01:38:09:10 01:38:12:12
Соседи в отчаянии	Desesperados, os vizinhos
	•
	01:38:13:14 01:38:16:12
и пожаловались властям.	chamaram as autoridades.
	•
	01:38:16:16 01:38:18:16
Они приходили,	Vieram,
	•
	01:38:19:06 01:38:21:02
звонили	tocaram à campainha,
	•
	01:38:23:10 01:38:25:00
и стучались в дверь,	bateram à porta,
	•
	01:38:26:00 01:38:28:16
но старики не открывали.	mas o casal de velhos não abria.

•
01:38:09:10
01:38:12:12
Les voisins étaient désespérés,

•
01:38:09:10
01:38:12:12
The neighbours were now desperate,

•
01:38:13:14
01:38:16:12
et ont appelé les autorités.

•
01:38:13:14
01:38:16:12
and called the authorities.

•
01:38:16:16
01:38:18:16
Des agents sont venus,

•
01:38:16:16
01:38:18:16
They came,

•
01:38:19:06
01:38:21:02
ont sonné,

•
01:38:19:06
01:38:21:02
rang the bell,

•
01:38:23:10
01:38:25:00
frappé à la porte,

•
01:38:23:10
01:38:25:00
banged on the door,

•
01:38:26:00
01:38:28:16
mais les vieux
n'ouvraient pas.

•
01:38:26:00
01:38:28:16
but the old couple wouldn't open.

	• 01:38:28:20 01:38:31:14
Время шло.	E assim tudo continuou na mesma.
	• 01:38:32:10 01:38:34:08
Власти приходили снова,	As autoridades voltaram,
	• 01:38:34:10 01:38:36:08
но старики так и не открывали дверь.	e eles continuaram a não abrir a porta.
	• 01:38:36:18 01:38:39:00
Однажды вечером, когда все садились ужинать,	Um dia, à hora do jantar,
	• 01:38:39:02 01:38:41:16
на лестнице раздался	ouviu-se nas escadas
	• 01:38:42:00 01:38:44:12
страшный душераздирающий вопль.	um grito horrível, lancinante.

•
01:38:28:20
01:38:31:14
Et cela a continué.

•
01:38:32:10
01:38:34:08
Les agents sont revenus

•
01:38:34:10
01:38:36:08
mais les vieux
n'ouvraient toujours pas.

•
01:38:36:18
01:38:39:00
Un soir,
à l'heure du dîner,

•
01:38:39:02
01:38:41:16
on a entendu dans les escaliers

•
01:38:42:00
01:38:44:12
un cri perçant, horrible.

•
01:38:28:20
01:38:31:14
And so it went on.

•
01:38:32:10
01:38:34:08
The authorities came back,

•
01:38:34:10
01:38:36:08
and still they wouldn't open the door.

•
01:38:36:18
01:38:39:00
One evening, at dinner-time,

•
01:38:39:02
01:38:41:16
a horrible, piercing scream

•
01:38:42:00
01:38:44:12
was heard in the stairs.

	• 01:38:45:10 01:38:47:18
Соседи бросились к дверям	Os vizinhos correram à porta
	• 01:38:49:02 01:38:51:00
и посмотрели вверх.	e olharam para cima.
	• 01:38:51:02 01:38:54:08
Там, на лестничной площадке сидела, согнувшись,	Lá em cima, no patamar, viram a velha
	• 01:38:55:08 01:38:57:06
старуха.	debruçada sobre alguma coisa.
	• 01:38:57:08 01:39:01:10
Соседи взбежали по ступенькам и увидели старика, лежащего на полу.	Os vizinhos subiram a correr e viram o velho no chão.
	• 01:39:03:10 01:39:04:24
Он был мёртв.	Estava morto.

•

01:38:45:10
01:38:47:18
Les voisins se sont précipités
vers leur porte

•

01:38:45:10
01:38:47:18
The neighbours rushed to their doors

•

01:38:49:02
01:38:51:00
et ont regardé en haut.

•

01:38:49:02
01:38:51:00
and looked up.

•

01:38:51:02
01:38:54:08
Là, sur le palier,
se tenait la vieille femme

•

01:38:51:02
01:38:54:08
There, on the landing,
was the old woman

•

01:38:55:08
01:38:57:06
accroupie près de quelque chose.

•

01:38:55:11
01:38:57:00
crouching over something.

•

01:38:57:08
01:39:01:10
Les voisins sont montés en courant
et ont vu le vieil homme sur le sol.

•

01:38:57:08
01:39:01:10
The neighbours rushed up
and saw the old man on the floor.

•

01:39:03:10
01:39:04:24
Il était mort.

•

01:39:03:10
01:39:04:24
He was dead.

	• 01:39:05:20 01:39:09:08
Дверь квартиры уже была закрыта.	A porta deles já tinha sido fechada.
	• 01:39:14:12 01:39:16:22
Кто-то вызвал скорую помощь.	Alguém chamou uma ambulância.
	• 01:39:18:00 01:39:21:22
Старуха молчаливо ждала посреди суматохи,	A velha esperou em silêncio no meio da barafunda,
	• 01:39:21:24 01:39:24:04
а потом уехала в машине,	e lá foi na ambulância
	• 01:39:24:06 01:39:27:16
увозившей и её мёртвого мужа.	com o seu marido morto.
	• 01:39:33:10 01:39:37:04
Соседи решили, что настала пора действовать.	Era altura de os vizinhos actuarem.

•

01:39:05:20
01:39:09:08
La porte de l'appartement
avait déjà été fermée.

•

01:39:14:12
01:39:16:22
Quelqu'un a appelé
une ambulance.

•

01:39:18:00
01:39:21:22
La vieille femme a attendu
en silence au milieu du brouhaha,

•

01:39:21:24
01:39:24:04
et est partie dans l'ambulance

•

01:39:24:06
01:39:27:16
avec son mari mort.

•

01:39:33:10
01:39:37:04
C'était le moment pour les voisins
de passer à l'action.

•

01:39:05:20
01:39:09:08
The door to the flat
had already been closed.

•

01:39:14:12
01:39:16:22
Someone rang an ambulance.

•

01:39:18:00
01:39:21:22
The old woman waited silently
amidst the commotion,

•

01:39:21:24
01:39:24:04
and went off in the ambulance

•

01:39:24:06
01:39:27:16
with her dead husband.

•

01:39:33:10
01:39:37:04
It was time
for the neighbours to act.

•

01:39:37:22
01:39:41:08

Задняя часть дома была покрыта лесами,

As traseiras do prédio estavam em obras,

•

01:39:41:10
01:39:44:00

так как там шёл ремонт.

havia um andaime montado.

•

01:39:44:18
01:39:46:02

Кто-то вскарабкался,

Alguém subiu,

•

01:39:46:12
01:39:48:00

взломал окно,

partiu um vidro da janela,

•

01:39:48:16
01:39:50:12

попал в квартиру,

entrou em casa deles,

•

01:39:50:16
01:39:52:00

открыл дверь,

abriu a porta,

•

01:39:37:22
01:39:41:08
L'arrière du bâtiment
était en cours de rénovation,

•

01:39:41:10
01:39:44:00
il y avait un échafaudage.

•

01:39:44:18
01:39:46:02
Quelqu'un l'a escaladé,

•

01:39:46:12
01:39:48:00
a cassé un carreau,

•

01:39:48:16
01:39:50:12
est entré dans l'appartement,

•

01:39:50:16
01:39:52:00
a ouvert la porte,

•

01:39:37:22
01:39:41:08
The back of the building
was being renovated,

•

01:39:41:10
01:39:44:00
there was a scaffold.

•

01:39:44:18
01:39:46:02
Someone went up,

•

01:39:46:12
01:39:48:00
broke a window pane,

•

01:39:48:16
01:39:50:12
got in the apartment,

•

01:39:50:16
01:39:52:00
opened the door,

	• 01:39:53:00 01:39:55:20
и тогда все увидели это.	e foi então que eles viram.
	• 01:40:00:16 01:40:03:22
Мусор, наваленный до потолка.	Havia lixo amontoado até ao tecto.
	• 01:40:04:18 01:40:07:02
Бесформенные груды мусора,	Montanhas de lixo sem forma definida,
	• 01:40:07:10 01:40:09:10
как на помойке.	como numa lixeira.
	• 01:40:09:20 01:40:11:00
Везде,	Por toda a parte,
	• 01:40:11:22 01:40:13:08
в каждой комнате,	em todas as divisões,

•
01:39:53:00
01:39:55:20
et là, ils l'ont vu.

•
01:39:53:00
01:39:55:20
and then they saw it.

•
01:40:00:16
01:40:03:22
Un énorme tas d'ordures
aussi haut que le plafond.

•
01:40:00:18
01:40:03:12
There was rubbish piled
as high as the ceiling.

•
01:40:04:18
01:40:07:02
Des montagnes d'ordures,
sans forme,

•
01:40:04:18
01:40:07:02
Shapeless mountains of rubbish,

•
01:40:07:10
01:40:09:10
comme dans un dépotoir.

•
01:40:07:10
01:40:09:02
like a rubbish dump.

•
01:40:09:20
01:40:11:00
Partout,

•
01:40:09:20
01:40:11:00
Everywhere,

•
01:40:11:22
01:40:13:08
dans chaque pièce,

•
01:40:11:22
01:40:13:08
in every room,

•
01:40:14:12
01:40:17:02

даже на кухне
и в ванной.

até mesmo na cozinha
e na casa de banho.

•
01:40:18:06
01:40:21:24

В мешках, которые старики
таскали,

Os sacos que tinham carregado
durante meses

•
01:40:22:02
01:40:24:16

был мусор,
вынесенный из домов на улицу,

tinham lixo doméstico
deixado na rua

•
01:40:24:18
01:40:26:20

чтобы «мусорка» подобрала его.

para o camião do lixo.

•
01:40:28:18
01:40:32:14

Соседи позвонили
в городскую санэпидстанцию.

Os vizinhos chamaram o serviço
de saneamento da cidade.

•
01:40:33:18
01:40:35:20

Приехал грузовик.

E veio um camião,

•
01:40:14:12
01:40:17:02
y compris la cuisine
et la salle de bains.

•
01:40:14:12
01:40:17:02
even in the kitchen
and the bathroom.

•
01:40:18:06
01:40:21:24
Ces sacs qu'ils avaient transportés
pendant des mois

•
01:40:18:06
01:40:21:24
Those bags they had carried
for months

•
01:40:22:02
01:40:24:16
contenaient les ordures
laissées sur le trottoir

•
01:40:22:02
01:40:24:12
contained household rubbish
left out in the street

•
01:40:24:18
01:40:26:20
pour être ramassées
par la benne.

•
01:40:24:18
01:40:27:04
for the rubbish truck.

•
01:40:28:18
01:40:32:14
Les voisins ont appelé
les services sanitaires de la ville.

•
01:40:28:18
01:40:32:14
The neighbours called
the sanitation department of the city.

•
01:40:33:18
01:40:35:20
Ils ont envoyé un camion,

•
01:40:33:18
01:40:35:20
And a truck came,

	• 01:40:37:06 01:40:39:22
Он возвращался трижды.	e fez três viagens.
	• 01:40:40:22 01:40:44:04
Его наполняли трижды, чтобы очистить квартиру.	Três levas para limpar o apartamento.
	• 01:40:49:06 01:40:51:08
Когда старуха вернулась,	Mais tarde, quando a velha voltou,
	• 01:40:51:10 01:40:54:00
соседи припали к дверным глазкам.	os vizinhos espreitaram-na pelos postigos.
	• 01:40:55:06 01:40:57:12
Она шла по ступенькам медленно,	A subir as escadas, devagar,
	• 01:40:59:02 01:41:01:10
медленнее, чем обычно.	mais devagar ainda do que era costume.

•
01:40:37:06
01:40:39:22
et il est revenu trois fois.

•
01:40:37:06
01:40:39:22
and it came back three times.

•
01:40:40:22
01:40:44:04
Il a fallu faire trois chargements
pour vider l'appartement.

•
01:40:40:22
01:40:44:04
It took three loads
to empty the apartment.

•
01:40:49:06
01:40:51:08
Lorsque la vieille femme
est revenue,

•
01:40:49:06
01:40:50:24
When the old woman came back later,

•
01:40:51:10
01:40:54:00
les voisins l'ont vue
par le judas de leur porte,

•
01:40:51:02
01:40:54:00
the neighbours saw her
from behind their peep-holes.

•
01:40:55:06
01:40:57:10
qui montait l'escalier,
lentement,

•
01:40:55:06
01:40:57:10
Going up the stairs,
slowly,

•
01:40:59:02
01:41:01:04
plus lentement que d'habitude.

•
01:40:59:02
01:41:01:04
slower than usual.

•

01:41:01:18
01:41:04:18

И они не решились
ничего сказать.

E não tiveram coragem
de lhe dizer fosse o que fosse.

•

01:41:11:16
01:41:13:16

Старика похоронили.

O velho foi enterrado.

•

01:41:13:20
01:41:16:06

Жизнь пошла своим чередом.

A vida continuou.

•

01:41:17:10
01:41:20:08

А старуха опять принялась за своё.

Mas a velha recomeçou.

•

01:41:21:10
01:41:22:22

Вскоре после похорон

Pouco tempo depois,

•

01:41:23:08
01:41:24:18

соседи увидели,

viram-na outra vez

•
01:41:01:18
01:41:04:18
Et ils n'ont pas eu le courage
de dire un mot.

•
01:41:01:18
01:41:04:18
And they didn't have the heart
to say a word.

•
01:41:11:16
01:41:13:16
Le vieil homme était enterré.

•
01:41:11:16
01:41:13:16
The old man was buried.

•
01:41:13:20
01:41:16:06
La vie continuait.

•
01:41:13:20
01:41:16:06
Life went on.

•
01:41:17:10
01:41:20:08
Mais la vieille femme
a recommencé.

•
01:41:17:10
01:41:20:08
But the old woman started again.

•
01:41:21:10
01:41:22:22
Très vite,

•
01:41:21:10
01:41:22:22
Soon after,

•
01:41:23:08
01:41:26:18
ils l'ont vue monter,
lentement, chez elle,

•
01:41:23:08
01:41:26:18
she was seen carrying
more plastic bags

	• 01:41:24:20 01:41:27:04
как она тащила новые мешки,	a acartar mais sacos de plástico,
	• 01:41:27:20 01:41:30:10
медленно поднимаясь по ступенькам.	lentamente, escadas acima.
	• 01:41:31:04 01:41:33:18
Она опять принялась за старое.	Tinha recomeçado tudo outra vez.
	• 01:41:40:02 01:41:43:00
Эта история была самой страшной	Esta história era a coisa mais horrível
	• 01:41:43:02 01:41:46:02
из всех, что я когда-либо слышал.	que eu alguma vez tinha ouvido.
	• 01:41:46:22 01:41:49:20
Страшнее, чем сказки о великанах,	Mais horrível do que as histórias de gigantes,

•
01:41:27:20
01:41:30:08
d'autres sacs en plastique.

•
01:41:27:20
01:41:30:08
slowly up the stairs.

•
01:41:31:04
01:41:33:18
Elle avait tout recommencé.

•
01:41:31:04
01:41:33:18
She had started again.

•
01:41:40:02
01:41:43:00
Cette histoire était la plus horrible

•
01:41:40:02
01:41:46:02
This story was more horrible
than anything I had ever heard.

•
01:41:43:02
01:41:46:02
que j'avais jamais entendue.

•
01:41:46:22
01:41:49:20
Plus que les histoires de géants,

•
01:41:46:22
01:41:49:20
More than stories of giants,

	•
	01:41:50:22
	01:41:53:20
о лебедях, превращаемых в девушек,	de cisnes a transformarem-se em donzelas,
	•
	01:41:54:06
	01:41:55:16
о привидениях	de fantasmas,
	•
	01:41:55:22
	01:41:57:24
и великих битвах.	ou de grandes batalhas.
	•
	01:41:59:00
	01:42:00:08
Для меня	Para mim,
	•
	01:42:00:10
	01:42:02:20
понятия о доме и чистоте	as noções de higiene e de lar
	•
	01:42:03:00
	01:42:04:14
были неразделимы.	eram inseparáveis.

•

01:41:50:22
01:41:53:20
de cygnes qui se transforment
en jeunes filles,

•

01:41:54:06
01:41:55:16
de fantômes,

•

01:41:55:22
01:41:57:24
et de grandes batailles.

•

01:41:59:00
01:42:00:08
Pour moi,

•

01:42:00:10
01:42:02:20
les notions de foyer
et d'hygiène

•

01:42:03:00
01:42:04:14
étaient inséparables.

•

01:41:50:22
01:41:53:20
swans turned into maidens,

•

01:41:54:06
01:41:55:16
ghosts,

•

01:41:55:22
01:41:57:24
and great battles.

•

01:41:59:04
01:42:00:02
To me,

•

01:42:00:04
01:42:02:20
the notions of home and hygiene

•

01:42:03:00
01:42:04:10
were inseparable.

	• 01:42:06:06 01:42:08:06
Дети бывают грязнулями,	As crianças podem ser sujas,
	• 01:42:09:04 01:42:13:16
но, в то же время, они более брезгливы, чем взрослые.	mas são também mais facilmente enojadas do que os adultos.
	• 01:42:14:22 01:42:17:18
Впервые я представлял себе мусор,	Pensei pela primeira vez em lixo,
	• 01:42:18:00 01:42:20:00
выброшенные объедки	nos restos abandonados,
	• 01:42:20:02 01:42:22:08
в огромном количестве.	como uma enorme quantidade.
	• 01:42:24:10 01:42:27:14
Миллионы тонн мусора во всём мире.	Nos milhões de toneladas de lixo no mundo.

•

01:42:06:06
01:42:08:06
Les enfants peuvent être sales,

•

01:42:06:06
01:42:08:06
Children may be dirty,

•

01:42:09:04
01:42:13:16
mais aussi plus facilement dégoûtés
que les adultes.

•

01:42:09:04
01:42:13:16
but also
more squeamish than adults.

•

01:42:14:22
01:42:17:18
Pour la première fois
je pensais aux ordures,

•

01:42:14:22
01:42:17:18
For the first time
I thought of rubbish,

•

01:42:18:00
01:42:20:00
aux restes que l'on jette

•

01:42:18:00
01:42:20:00
of discarded leftovers

•

01:42:20:02
01:42:22:08
comme à une immense quantité.

•

01:42:20:02
01:42:22:08
as an immense quantity.

•

01:42:24:10
01:42:27:14
Des millions de tonnes d'ordures
dans le monde.

•

01:42:24:10
01:42:27:08
The millions of tons of rubbish
in the world.

	•
	01:42:29:18
	01:42:32:08
Новая,	Uma visão nova
	da vida,
	•
	01:42:32:10
	01:42:33:24
более глобальная,	mais global,
	•
	01:42:34:02
	01:42:35:18
более пугающая	mais aterradora,
	•
	01:42:35:20
	01:42:37:10
и более грязная картина жизни.	mais suja.
	•
	01:42:42:02
	01:42:43:16
Я смотрел на Байкал,	Olhei para o Baikal,

•
01:42:29:18
01:42:30:14
Une nouvelle

•
01:42:29:18
01:42:30:14
A new,

•
01:42:30:16
01:42:32:08
vision de la vie,

•
01:42:30:16
01:42:32:06
more global,

•
01:42:32:10
01:42:33:24
plus globale,

•
01:42:32:12
01:42:33:20
more frightening,

•
01:42:34:02
01:42:35:18
plus effrayante,

•
01:42:34:06
01:42:37:04
dirtier vision of life.

•
01:42:35:20
01:42:37:10
plus sale.

•
01:42:42:02
01:42:43:16
Je regardais le Baïkal,

•
01:42:42:02
01:42:43:16
I looked at the Baikal,

	• 01:42:43:18 01:42:46:00
огромный и глубокий.	enorme e profundo.
	• 01:42:46:10 01:42:48:06
И я придумал план.	E inventei um plano.
	• 01:42:54:12 01:42:56:04
Байкал может вместить	O Baikal poderia conter
	• 01:42:56:06 01:42:58:04
весь мусор Земли.	todo o lixo do mundo.
	• 01:42:59:04 01:43:02:10
Я представлял, как отовсюду будут прилетать самолёты	Imaginava que viriam aviões de toda a parte
	• 01:43:02:12 01:43:05:20
с огромными мешками мусора	com grandes sacos de lixo

•
01:42:43:18
01:42:46:00
immense et profond.

•
01:42:43:18
01:42:46:00
huge and deep.

•
01:42:46:10
01:42:48:06
Et j'élaborais un plan.

•
01:42:46:10
01:42:48:06
And I devised a plan.

•
01:42:54:12
01:42:56:04
Le Baïkal pouvait contenir

•
01:42:54:12
01:42:56:04
The Baikal could take

•
01:42:56:06
01:42:58:04
les ordures du monde entier.

•
01:42:56:06
01:42:58:04
all the rubbish of the world.

•
01:42:59:04
01:43:02:10
J'imaginais des avions
arrivant de partout

•
01:42:59:04
01:43:02:10
I imagined that planes
from everywhere

•
01:43:02:12
01:43:05:20
avec d'immenses sacs d'ordures

•
01:43:02:12
01:43:05:20
would come with big bags of rubbish

•

01:43:06:04
01:43:09:08

и будут бросать их в Байкал. para os descarregarem ali.

•

01:43:10:04
01:43:12:10

Мусор будет тонуть Que os sacos
se afundariam

•

01:43:12:12
01:43:14:14

и исчезать навсегда. e nunca mais seriam vistos.

•

01:43:19:22
01:43:23:20

Длина Байкала - 556 километров, O Baikal tem 556 km
de comprimento,

•

01:43:24:10
01:43:28:04

ширина - 44 километра. e 44 km de largura.

•

01:43:28:24
01:43:32:04

Места в нём хватит на много веков. Havia espaço
para muitos séculos.

•

01:43:06:04
01:43:09:08
pour les y jeter.

•

01:43:10:04
01:43:12:10
Ils couleraient,

•

01:43:12:12
01:43:14:08
et personne ne les reverrait plus.

•

01:43:19:22
01:43:23:20
Le Baïkal
fait 556 km de long,

•

01:43:24:10
01:43:28:04
et 44 km de large.

•

01:43:28:24
01:43:32:04
Cela suffirait
pour plusieurs siècles.

•

01:43:06:04
01:43:09:08
to drop them there.

•

01:43:10:04
01:43:12:10
They would sink,

•

01:43:12:12
01:43:14:08
never to be seen again.

•

01:43:19:22
01:43:23:20
The Baikal is 556 km long,

•

01:43:24:10
01:43:28:04
and 44 km across.

•

01:43:28:24
01:43:32:04
There was room for many centuries.

•

01:43:33:14
01:43:35:02

Я воображал самолёты, — Imaginei os aviões

•

01:43:35:04
01:43:37:10

кружащие над Байкалом. — a sobrevoar o Baikal.

•

01:43:37:18
01:43:39:20

Шум их моторов, — O ruído dos motores,

•

01:43:40:02
01:43:42:20

флаги, нарисованные на хвостах, — as bandeiras pintadas
nas caudas

•

01:43:43:02
01:43:44:20

и разноцветные мешки, — e sacos coloridos

•

01:43:44:24
01:43:47:12

падающие с огромной высоты. — a cairem de grandes alturas.

•

01:43:33:14
01:43:35:02
J'imaginais les avions

•

01:43:33:14
01:43:35:02
I imagined the planes

•

01:43:35:04
01:43:37:10
tournant au-dessus du Baïkal.

•

01:43:35:04
01:43:37:10
circling the Baikal.

•

01:43:37:18
01:43:39:20
Le bruit des moteurs,

•

01:43:37:18
01:43:39:20
The noise of their engines,

•

01:43:40:02
01:43:42:20
les drapeaux peints
sur leur queue,

•

01:43:40:02
01:43:42:20
the flags painted on their tails,

•

01:43:43:02
01:43:44:20
et des sacs colorés

•

01:43:43:02
01:43:44:20
and colourful bags

•

01:43:44:24
01:43:47:12
largués à haute altitude.

•

01:43:44:24
01:43:47:12
falling from great heights.

•

01:43:48:10
01:43:51:08

Байкал превратился бы в важный

O Baikal seria
um importante centro,

•

01:43:51:10
01:43:53:04

международный

internacional

•

01:43:53:06
01:43:54:16

многонациональный центр.

e cosmopolita.

•

01:43:55:20
01:43:58:18

Я воображал, что я начальник

Imaginei-me
a mim próprio comandante

•

01:43:58:20
01:44:01:20

контрольной вышки этого аэропорта,

da torre deste aeroporto

•
01:43:48:10
01:43:50:14
Le Baïkal serait

•
01:43:48:10
01:43:50:14
The Baikal would be an important,

•
01:43:50:16
01:43:51:18
un centre important,

•
01:43:50:16
01:43:51:18
international,

•
01:43:51:20
01:43:53:04
international,

•
01:43:51:20
01:43:54:14
cosmopolitan centre.

•
01:43:53:06
01:43:54:16
cosmopolite.

•
01:43:55:20
01:43:58:18
Je m'imaginais contrôlant

•
01:43:55:20
01:43:58:18
I imagined myself the commander

•
01:43:58:20
01:44:01:20
la tour de cet aéroport

•
01:43:58:20
01:44:01:20
of the tower of this airport

•

01:44:02:18
01:44:05:02

где самолёты никогда не садятся.

onde os aviões
nunca aterrariam.

•

01:44:07:00
01:44:09:02

Мне и в голову не приходило,

Não me ocorreu sequer

•

01:44:09:04
01:44:12:10

что я придумывал
экологическое бедствие.

o desastre ecológico
que estava a criar.

•

01:44:13:16
01:44:16:12

В школе я узнал, что

Tinha aprendido na escola
que um número incalculável de

•

01:44:16:14
01:44:18:08

Epischura baicalensis,

Epischura baicalensis,

•

01:44:18:20
01:44:21:10

мельчайшие рачки,
в бессчётном количестве

um camarão minúsculo,

•
01:44:02:18
01:44:05:02
où les avions
n'atterriraient jamais.

•
01:44:01:22
01:44:05:02
where planes would never land.

•
01:44:07:00
01:44:10:00
Il ne m'est pas venu à l'esprit

•
01:44:07:00
01:44:10:00
It didn't cross my mind

•
01:44:10:02
01:44:13:06
que j'étais en train de créer
un désastre écologique.

•
01:44:10:02
01:44:13:06
the ecological disaster
I was creating.

•
01:44:14:00
01:44:16:12
J'avais appris à l'école
que d'innombrables

•
01:44:14:00
01:44:16:12
I had learnt in school
that countless numbers of

•
01:44:16:14
01:44:18:08
Epischura baicalensis,

•
01:44:16:14
01:44:18:08
Epischura baicalensis,

•
01:44:18:16
01:44:21:12
une espèce de minuscules crevettes,

•
01:44:18:16
01:44:21:12
a tiny shrimp,

•

01:44:22:04
01:44:24:08

постоянно очищают Байкал,

purifica incessantemente
o Baikal,

•

01:44:24:10
01:44:27:08

поедая водоросли и бактерии.

alimentando-se
de algas e bactérias.

•

01:44:29:02
01:44:32:20

Сейчас построенный на Ангаре
целлюлозный завод

Agora a fábrica de celulose
no Angara

•

01:44:33:00
01:44:35:18

выбрасывает отходы в Байкал.

deita o seu lixo no Baikal.

•

01:44:37:10
01:44:38:22

Правительство говорит,

O governo disse

•

01:44:38:24
01:44:41:18

что целлюлоза нужна

que a celulose era necessária

•

01:44:22:04
01:44:24:08
nettoyaient le Baïkal
en permanence

•

01:44:22:04
01:44:24:08
forever cleanse the Baikal

•

01:44:24:10
01:44:27:08
en se nourrissant d'algues
et de bactéries.

•

01:44:24:10
01:44:27:08
by feeding on algae
and bacteria.

•

01:44:29:02
01:44:32:20
Maintenant l'usine de cellulose
sur l'Angara

•

01:44:29:02
01:44:31:06
Now the cellulose plant
on the Angara

•

01:44:33:00
01:44:35:18
déverse ses déchets
dans le Baïkal.

•

01:44:31:08
01:44:35:14
pours its rubbish into the Baikal.

•

01:44:37:10
01:44:38:22
Le gouvernement a dit

•

01:44:37:10
01:44:38:22
The government said

•

01:44:38:24
01:44:41:18
qu'on avait besoin de la cellulose

•

01:44:38:24
01:44:41:18
the cellulose was needed

•

01:44:41:20
01:44:44:24

для создания более прочных
самолётных шин.

para fazer pneus de avião
mais resistentes.

•

01:44:50:12
01:44:52:00

Позже,

Foi mais tarde,

•

01:44:52:02
01:44:54:16

много позже моей любви к Ольге,

muito depois
de eu ter amado a Olga,

•

01:44:55:04
01:44:58:12

в то время, когда я открывал для
себя подростковую любовь,

quando começava a descobrir
o amor adolescente,

•

01:44:59:16
01:45:01:12

я решил, что те старики

que me lembrei
do tal casal de velhos

•

01:45:01:14
01:45:03:22

были парой влюблённых.

como duas pessoas
que se amaram.

•

01:44:41:20
01:44:44:24
pour produire des pneus
plus résistants pour les avions.

•

01:44:41:20
01:44:44:24
for stronger aeroplane tires.

•

01:44:50:12
01:44:52:00
C'est plus tard,

•

01:44:50:12
01:44:52:00
It was later,

•

01:44:52:02
01:44:54:16
bien après avoir aimé Olga,

•

01:44:52:02
01:44:54:16
long after I loved Olga,

•

01:44:55:04
01:44:58:12
à l'époque où je découvrais
les amours adolescents,

•

01:44:55:04
01:44:58:12
at a time when I was discovering
teenage love,

•

01:44:59:16
01:45:01:12
que j'ai pensé
à ce couple de vieux

•

01:44:59:16
01:45:01:06
that those old people

•

01:45:01:14
01:45:03:22
comme à des amoureux.

•

01:45:01:08
01:45:03:19
came back to me
as lovers.

	• 01:45:05:12 01:45:06:22
Я спрашивал себя,	Perguntei-me
	• 01:45:06:24 01:45:08:08
когда и как	quando, como
	• 01:45:08:10 01:45:11:06
начали они заполнять свой дом	começaram eles a encher a sua casa
	• 01:45:11:08 01:45:14:10
мусором из домов незнакомцев.	com os restos de vidas anónimas.
	• 01:45:15:14 01:45:18:20
А, может быть, наоборот,	Mas talvez não fossem anónimas.
	• 01:45:18:22 01:45:21:04
они собирали мусор,	Talvez apanhassem o lixo

•
01:45:05:12
01:45:06:22
Je me demandais

•
01:45:05:12
01:45:06:22
I asked myself

•
01:45:06:24
01:45:08:08
quand, comment

•
01:45:06:24
01:45:08:08
when, how

•
01:45:08:10
01:45:11:06
ils avaient commencé à remplir
leur appartement

•
01:45:08:10
01:45:11:06
did they start filling their home

•
01:45:11:08
01:45:14:10
avec les restes
de vies anonymes.

•
01:45:11:08
01:45:14:10
with the leftovers
from anonymous lives.

•
01:45:15:14
01:45:18:20
Mais peut-être
n'étaient elles pas anonymes.

•
01:45:15:14
01:45:18:20
But perhaps
they were not anonymous.

•
01:45:18:22
01:45:21:04
Peut-être qu'ils ramassaient
les ordures

•
01:45:18:22
01:45:22:14
Maybe they collected the rubbish
of people they knew.

•

01:45:21:06
01:45:23:02

выбрасываемый людьми,
которых они знали.

de pessoas que conheciam.

•

01:45:24:00
01:45:26:08

Проработав всю жизнь на почте,

Talvez que depois
de uma vida nos correios,

•

01:45:26:12
01:45:29:08

сортируя запечатанные письма,

a separar correspondência
que não abriam,

•

01:45:29:14
01:45:32:16

возможно, они искали
чужие секреты.

estivessem à procura
de segredos.

•

01:45:33:18
01:45:36:00

Ленты от подарочных свёртков,

Fitas de embrulhar presentes,

•

01:45:36:16
01:45:38:02

лекарства,

remédios,

•
01:45:21:06
01:45:23:02
des gens qu'ils connaissaient.

•
01:45:24:00
01:45:26:08
Peut-être qu'après avoir
passé leur vie à la Poste,

•
01:45:24:00
01:45:26:08
Perhaps that
after a life at the Post Office,

•
01:45:26:12
01:45:29:08
à trier du courrier
qu'ils n'ouvraient pas,

•
01:45:26:12
01:45:29:08
sorting out mail they did not open,

•
01:45:29:14
01:45:32:16
ils recherchaient des secrets.

•
01:45:29:14
01:45:32:16
they were seeking secrets.

•
01:45:33:18
01:45:36:00
Les rubans de cadeaux,

•
01:45:33:18
01:45:36:00
Ribbons from presents,

•
01:45:36:16
01:45:38:02
des médicaments,

•
01:45:36:16
01:45:38:02
medicines,

	•
	01:45:38:12 01:45:40:06
разорванные письма,	cartas rasgadas,
	•
	01:45:40:22 01:45:42:22
разбитую посуду,	louça partida,
	•
	01:45:43:04 01:45:44:24
остатки еды,	comida,
	•
	01:45:45:14 01:45:46:16
волосы,	cabelo,
	•
	01:45:46:18 01:45:48:16
обрезки ногтей,	unhas cortadas,
	•
	01:45:49:14 01:45:52:04
размытое полужидкое месиво	pastas indistintas, meio-líquidas,

•

01:45:38:12
01:45:40:06
des lettres déchirées,

•

01:45:40:22
01:45:42:22
de la vaisselle cassée,

•

01:45:43:04
01:45:44:24
de la nourriture,

•

01:45:45:14
01:45:46:16
des cheveux,

•

01:45:46:18
01:45:48:16
des rognures d'ongle,

•

01:45:49.14
01:45:52:04
des matières pâteuses indéterminées, semi-liquides,

•

01:45:38:12
01:45:40:06
torn letters,

•

01:45:40:22
01:45:42:22
broken crockery,

•

01:45:43:04
01:45:44:24
food,

•

01:45:45:14
01:45:46:16
hair,

•

01:45:46:18
01:45:48:16
nail clippings,

•

01:45:49:14
01:45:52:04
indistinct, half liquid pastes

	• 01:45:52:06 01:45:54:12
плесени и гниения.	bolorentas e putrefactas.
	• 01:45:59:04 01:46:02:10
Как они переходили из одной комнаты в другую?	Como passariam de uma divisão a outra?
	• 01:46:03:12 01:46:04:24
Перешагивая,	Andando por cima,
	• 01:46:05:04 01:46:06:06
давя,	esborrachando,
	• 01:46:06:20 01:46:09:02
взбираясь на груды мусора?	subindo montanhas de lixo?
	• 01:46:10:20 01:46:14:18
Может быть, они прокладывали тропинки между комнатами?	Teriam feito carreiros a ligar as divisões?

•
01:45:52:06
01:45:54:12
moisies et putréfiées.

•
01:45:52:06
01:45:54:12
of mould and putrefaction.

•
01:45:59:04
01:46:02:10
Comment faisaient-ils
pour passer d'une pièce à l'autre ?

•
01:45:59:04
01:46:02:10
How did they move
from one room to another?

•
01:46:03:12
01:46:04:24
En enjambant,

•
01:46:03:12
01:46:04:24
By stepping over,

•
01:46:05:04
01:46:06:06
écrasant,

•
01:46:05:04
01:46:06:06
squashing,

•
01:46:06:20
01:46:09:02
escaladant
des montagnes d'ordures ?

•
01:46:06:20
01:46:09:02
climbing mountains of rubbish?

•
01:46:10:20
01:46:14:18
Avaient-ils laissé des chemins
reliant leurs pièces ?

•
01:46:10:20
01:46:14:18
Did they leave paths
connecting their rooms?

	• 01:46:17:06 01:46:18:12
Считали ли они нужным	Se cozinhavam,
	• 01:46:18:14 01:46:20:08
мыть продукты,	teria alguma importância para eles
	• 01:46:20:12 01:46:22:12
если они готовили пищу?	que lavassem os alimentos antes de os cozinhar?
	• 01:46:23:16 01:46:25:10
Мыли ли они посуду	Quando acabavam de comer,
	• 01:46:25:12 01:46:27:08
после еды?	lavariam a loiça?
	• 01:46:28:04 01:46:32:00
Где они провели черту	Haveria para eles alguma linha divisória

•

01:46:17:06
01:46:18:12
S'ils cuisinaient,

•

01:46:17:06
01:46:18:12
If they cooked,

•

01:46:18:14
01:46:20:08
est-ce qu'il était important
pour eux

•

01:46:18:14
01:46:20:02
did it matter to them

•

01:46:20:12
01:46:22:12
de laver les aliments
avant de les cuire ?

•

01:46:20:04
01:46:22:12
that food was washed before cooking?

•

01:46:23:16
01:46:25:10
Lorsqu'ils avaient fini
de manger,

•

01:46:23:16
01:46:25:04
When they finished eating,

•

01:46:25:12
01:46:27:08
faisaient-ils la vaisselle ?

•

01:46:25:06
01:46:27:02
did they wash up?

•

01:46:28:04
01:46:32:00
Où fixaient-ils la limite

•

01:46:28:04
01:46:32:00
Where did they draw the line

	•
	01:46:32:12
	01:46:34:02
между тем, что их окружало	entre o que os rodeava
	•
	01:46:34:04
	01:46:35:16
и образом жизни, который они вели	e os hábitos quotidianos que tiveram
	•
	01:46:35:18
	01:46:38:10
до того, как их жизнь изменилась?	antes da mudança nas suas vidas?
	•
	01:46:42:12
	01:46:44:00
Где они ели?	Onde comeriam eles?
	•
	01:46:44:12
	01:46:45:22
За столом?	A uma mesa?
	•
	01:46:47:02
	01:46:50:04
За столом посреди гниющих остатков	Uma mesa no meio de comida apodrecida,

•
01:46:32:12
01:46:34:12
entre leur environnement

•
01:46:32:12
01:46:34:12
between their surroundings

•
01:46:34:14
01:46:36:12
et leurs habitudes quotidiennes

•
01:46:34:14
01:46:36:12
and the daily habits they had

•
01:46:36:14
01:46:38:14
avant que leur vie ne change ?

•
01:46:36:14
01:46:38:14
before their lives changed?

•
01:46:42:12
01:46:44:00
Où mangeaient-ils ?

•
01:46:42:12
01:46:44:00
Where did they eat?

•
01:46:44:12
01:46:45:22
A table ?

•
01:46:44:12
01:46:45:22
At a table?

•
01:46:47:02
01:46:49:20
Une table au milieu de restes
en décomposition

•
01:46:47:02
01:46:49:10
A table amid the decomposing food

•

01:46:50:18
01:46:52:20

еды других? | vinda das refeições de outros?

•

01:46:53:04
01:46:54:12

На полу? | No chão?

•

01:46:55:02
01:46:56:14

На мусоре? | No lixo?

•

01:47:00:22
01:47:02:22

Мылись ли они? | Lavar-se-iam?

•

01:47:03:22
01:47:06:10

Меняли ли одежду? | Mudariam de roupa?

•

01:47:06:24
01:47:09:12

Стирали ли одежду? | Lavariam a roupa?

•

01:46:50:20
01:46:52:20
jetés par d'autres
à la fin des repas ?

•

01:46:49:12
01:46:52:10
from the meals of others?

•

01:46:53:04
01:46:54:12
Sur le sol ?

•

01:46:53:04
01:46:54:12
On the floor?

•

01:46:55:02
01:46:56:14
Sur les ordures ?

•

01:46:55:02
01:46:56:14
On the rubbish?

•

01:47:00:22
01:47:02:22
Se lavaient-ils ?

•

01:47:00:22
01:47:02:22
Did they wash themselves?

•

01:47:03:22
01:47:06:10
Se changeaient-ils ?

•

01:47:03:22
01:47:06:10
Did they change their clothes?

•

01:47:06:24
01:47:09:12
Lavaient-ils leurs vêtements ?

•

01:47:06:24
01:47:09:12
Did they wash their clothes?

•

01:47:13:16
01:47:15:08

Где они спали?

Onde dormiriam?

•

01:47:20:06
01:47:23:14

Нравилась ли им
компания мышей и крыс?

Seria que gostavam da companhia
de ratos e ratazanas?

•

01:47:24:22
01:47:28:06

Были ли они их друзьями
или питомцами?

Como animais de estimação,
como amigos?

•

01:47:33:12
01:47:35:06

Углекислый газ,

Anidrido carbónico,

•

01:47:35:20
01:47:38:00

запах сероводорода,

gas sulfídrico,

•

01:47:38:02
01:47:40:02

метана и аммония

metano e amoníaco

•
01:47:13:16
01:47:15:08
Où dormaient-ils ?

•
01:47:13:16
01:47:15:08
Where did they sleep?

•
01:47:20:06
01:47:23:14
Appréciaient-ils
la compagnie des rats et des souris ?

•
01:47:20:06
01:47:23:14
Did they enjoy
the company of mice and rats?

•
01:47:24:22
01:47:28:06
Comme animaux domestiques,
comme amis ?

•
01:47:24:22
01:47:28:06
As pets, as friends?

•
01:47:33:12
01:47:35:06
Le dioxyde de carbone,

•
01:47:33:12
01:47:35:06
Carbon dioxide,

•
01:47:35:20
01:47:38:00
l'acide hydrosulphurique,

•
01:47:35:20
01:47:38:00
hydrogen sulphide,

•
01:47:38:02
01:47:40:02
le méthane et l'ammonium

•
01:47:38:02
01:47:40:02
methane and ammonium

	•
	01:47:40:04 01:47:41:20
окружал их.	eram os cheiros à sua volta.
	•
	01:47:42:06 01:47:44:12
Запах кошачьей мочи.	O cheiro de mijo de gato.
	•
	01:47:49:22 01:47:52:10
Углерод, азот и влага,	Carbono, azoto e humidade,
	•
	01:47:52:20 01:47:55:16
способствующие размножению микроорганизмов.	criando microrganismos.
	•
	01:47:56:12 01:47:59:12
Брожение на вершинах мусорных куч.	Fermentações aeróbicas nas camadas superiores do lixo.
	•
	01:48:00:10 01:48:03:18
В глубине этих куч, без воздуха,	No interior dessas montanhas, onde o ar não penetrava,

•
01:47:40:04
01:47:41:20
étaient les odeurs qui
les entouraient.

•
01:47:40:04
01:47:41:20
were the smells
that surrounded them.

•
01:47:42:06
01:47:44:12
L'odeur de pisse de chat.

•
01:47:42:06
01:47:44:12
The smell of cat piss.

•
01:47:49:22
01:47:52:10
Le carbone, l'azote et l'humidité

•
01:47:49:22
01:47:52:10
Carbon, nitrogen, and moisture

•
01:47:52:20
01:47:55:16
qui favorisaient le développement
de micro-organismes.

•
01:47:52:20
01:47:55:16
brewing microorganisms.

•
01:47:56:12
01:47:59:12
Les fermentations aérobies sur
les couches supérieures des ordures.

•
01:47:56:12
01:47:59:06
Aerobic fermentations
on the top layers of rubbish.

•
01:48:00:10
01:48:02:20
Au plus profond de ces montagnes,

•
01:48:00:10
01:48:02:20
Deep in those mountains,

	• 01:48:03:20 01:48:05:20
размножаются бактерии и грибки,	bactérias e fungos a crescer
	• 01:48:06:08 01:48:08:10
вырабатывая тепло.	e a produzir calor.
	• 01:48:09:14 01:48:11:22
Зимой им никогда не было холодно.	Se era Inverno, eles nunca tinham frio.
	• 01:48:18:06 01:48:21:08
Когда я учился в Ленинградском театральном институте,	No Instituto Teatral de S. Petersburgo,
	• 01:48:22:08 01:48:23:22
мне надо было представить	quando tive de apresentar

•
01:48:02:22
01:48:04:10
à l'abri de l'air,

•
01:48:02:22
01:48:04:10
closed off from the air,

•
01:48:04:12
01:48:06:18
des bactéries et des champignons
se multipliaient,

•
01:48:04:12
01:48:08:04
bacteria and fungi growing
and producing heat.

•
01:48:06:20
01:48:08:10
produisant de la chaleur.

•
01:48:09:14
01:48:11:22
En hiver,
ils n'avaient jamais froid.

•
01:48:09:14
01:48:11:22
If it was winter,
they were never cold.

•
01:48:18:06
01:48:21:08
A l'institut théâtral de Leningrad,

•
01:48:18:06
01:48:21:08
At the Leningrad Theatrical Institute,

•
01:48:22:08
01:48:26:10
lorsque j'ai dû présenter
mon premier projet de film,

•
01:48:22:08
01:48:26:10
when I had to present
my first film project,

	• 01:48:24:00 01:48:26:10
мой первый дипломный фильм.	o meu primeiro projecto cinematográfico,
	• 01:48:27:20 01:48:31:16
Моим сценарием был рассказ об этих стариках.	o meu guião era a história do casal de velhos.
	• 01:48:33:08 01:48:37:02
Я нашёл актёров, старую квартиру...	Tinha os actores, um apartamento antigo...
	• 01:48:37:20 01:48:40:16
Но институт не принял мой проект.	Mas o meu projecto foi rejeitado pela escola.
	• 01:48:41:14 01:48:42:14
Это означало,	Isto faria
	• 01:48:42:16 01:48:46:04
что их призраки будут по-прежнему преследовать меня.	com que os dois velhos continuassem a assombrar-me.

•

01:48:27:20
01:48:31:16
j'ai repris dans mon script
l'histoire du vieux couple.

•

01:48:27:20
01:48:31:16
the old couple's story
was my script.

•

01:48:33:08
01:48:37:02
J'avais les acteurs,
un vieil appartement...

•

01:48:33:08
01:48:37:02
I had the actors,
an old apartment...

•

01:48:37:20
01:48:40:16
Mais mon projet
a été rejeté par l'école.

•

01:48:37:20
01:48:40:16
Yet my project
was rejected by the school.

•

01:48:41:14
01:48:42:14
Cela voulait dire

•

01:48:41:14
01:48:42:14
This meant

•

01:48:42:16
01:48:46:04
qu'ils continueraient
à me hanter.

•

01:48:42.16
01:48:46:04
that they would continue
to haunt me.

	•
	01:48:46:24
	01:48:50:02
Я мог выбросить из головы детскую фантазию	Podia libertar-me da minha fantasia de criança,
	•
	01:48:50:04
	01:48:52:02
о Байкале, как о всемирной самоочищающейся	do Baikal como a lixeira do mundo
	•
	01:48:52:04
	01:48:54:18
мусорной свалке,	que continuamente se purificava,
	•
	01:48:55:16
	01:48:57:12
но я не мог забыть,	mas não podia esquecer
	•
	01:48:57:14
	01:48:59:16
что они любили друг друга,	que eles se tinham amado,
	•
	01:49:00:08
	01:49:01:08
трогали друг друга,	tocado,

•
01:48:46:24
01:48:50:02
Je pouvais bien renoncer
à cette lubie d'enfant

•
01:48:46:24
01:48:50:02
I could dismiss my childhood fantasy

•
01:48:50:04
01:48:52:02
de transformer le Baïkal

•
01:48:52:04
01:48:54:18
en dépotoir mondial
capable de s'auto-purifier,

•
01:48:50:04
01:48:54:18
of the Baikal as the world's
self-purifying rubbish dump

•
01:48:55:16
01:48:57:12
mais je ne pouvais pas oublier

•
01:48:55:16
01:48:57:12
but I couldn't forget

•
01:48:57:14
01:48:59:16
qu'ils s'étaient aimés,

•
01:48:57:14
01:48:59:16
that they loved each other,

•
01:49:00:08
01:49:01:08
touchés,

•
01:49:00:08
01:49:01:08
touched,

	•
	01:49:01:10 01:49:02:10
целовались	beijado,
	•
	01:49:02:18 01:49:07:20
на гниющих отбросах из домов других людей.	sobre os restos putrefactos dos outros.
	•
	01:49:08:10 01:49:11:24
Что их жизнь в этой низости была пактом.	Que a sua vida na abjecção era um pacto.
	•
	01:49:13:04 01:49:15:12
Что это была история любви	Que a sua história era uma história de amor
	•
	01:49:15:14 01:49:18:02
на необитаемом острове	numa ilha deserta
	•
	01:49:18:08 01:49:20:06
за закрытой дверью.	atrás de uma porta fechada.

•
01:49:01:10
01:49:02:10
embrassés,

•
01:49:01:10
01:49:02:10
kissed,

•
01:49:02:18
01:49:07:20
sur les déchets en décomposition
des autres.

•
01:49:02:18
01:49:07:20
on the putrefying rejects of others.

•
01:49:08:10
01:49:11:24
Que leur vie dans l'abjection
était un pacte.

•
01:49:08:10
01:49:11:24
That their life in abjection
was a pact.

•
01:49:13:04
01:49:15:12
Que leur histoire était
une histoire d'amour

•
01:49:13:04
01:49:15:12
That theirs was a love story

•
01:49:15:14
01:49:18:02
sur une île déserte

•
01:49:15:14
01:49:18:02
on a desert island

•
01:49:18:08
01:49:20:06
derrière une porte close.

•
01:49:18:08
01:49:20:06
behind a closed door.

•

01:49:21:08
01:49:24:00

Как дети, увлекшиеся игрой,

Como crianças a brincar,

•

01:49:24:12
01:49:27:16

они были далеки от всех остальных.

estavam longe de toda a gente.

•

01:49:29:02
01:49:31:08

Как все старики, они боялись,

Como velhos,
viviam com o medo

•

01:49:32:08
01:49:34:22

что один из них умрёт первым.

de que um deles
morresse primeiro.

•

01:49:40:16
01:49:44:00

Моё желание сделать фильм
об этом пропало.

Eu já nem queria fazer o filme.

•

01:49:44:20
01:49:47:14

Но всякий раз, когда я видел
влюблённых

Mas sempre que via amor,

•

01:49:21:08
01:49:24:00
Comme les enfants
lorsqu'ils jouent,

•

01:49:21:08
01:49:24:00
Like children at play,

•

01:49:24:12
01:49:27:16
ils s'étaient coupés du monde.

•

01:49:24:12
01:49:27:16
they were far from everyone else.

•

01:49:29:02
01:49:31:08
Comme vieux,
ils avaient peur

•

01:49:32:08
01:49:34:22
que l'un d'eux meure le premier.

•

01:49:29:02
01:49:34:08
As old people they were frightened
that one of them would die first.

•

01:49:40:16
01:49:44:00
Je ne voulais même plus
faire ce film.

•

01:49:40:16
01:49:44:00
I didn't even want
to do the film anymore.

•

01:49:44:20
01:49:47:14
Mais chaque fois que
je voyais l'amour,

•

01:49:44:20
01:49:47:14
But whenever I saw love,

•

01:49:47:16
01:49:49:18

или кучу мусора, | ou lixo,

•

01:49:50:00
01:49:51:16

я думал о них. | lá estavam eles.

•

01:49:58:12
01:50:00:22

Я стал режиссёром монтажа. | Dedique-me à montagem cinematográfica.

•

01:50:02:04
01:50:03:04

Много лет спустя | Anos depois,

•

01:50:03:06
01:50:07:16

я был приглашён
на кинофестиваль в Лукарно.

fui convidado para um festival
de cinema em Locarno.

•

01:50:08:16
01:50:12:14

Это была моя первая поездка
за границу.

Era a minha primeira
saída ao estrangeiro.

•
01:49:47:16
01:49:49:18
ou des ordures,

•
01:49:47:16
01:49:49:18
or rubbish,

•
01:49:50:00
01:49:51:16
ils étaient là.

•
01:49:50:00
01:49:51:16
they were there.

•
01:49:58:12
01:50:00:22
Je suis devenu monteur.

•
01:49:58:12
01:50:00:22
I became a film-editor.

•
01:50:02:04
01:50:03:04
Des années plus tard,

•
01:50:02:04
01:50:03:04
Years later,

•
01:50:03:06
01:50:07:16
j'ai été invité à un festival du film
à Locarno.

•
01:50:03:06
01:50:07:16
I was invited
to a film festival in Locarno.

•
01:50:08:16
01:50:12:14
C'était mon premier
voyage à l'étranger.

•
01:50:08:16
01:50:12:14
It was my first time abroad.

	•
	01:50:15:06
	01:50:17:00
С помощью Армандо,	Com a ajuda do Armando,
	•
	01:50:17:04
	01:50:19:18
моего нового друга из Рима,	um amigo novo, de Roma,
	•
	01:50:22:22
	01:50:25:18
с которым я познакомился на фестивале,	que tinha conhecido no festival,
	•
	01:50:27:02
	01:50:31:14
я смог отыскать след итальянского друга моего отца,	consegui descobrir o rasto do amigo italiano do meu pai,
	•
	01:50:32:04
	01:50:33:06
Нино,	Nino,
	•
	01:50:34:02
	01:50:36:16
рассказавшего историю о стариках.	que lhe tinha contado a história dos velhos.

•

01:50:15:06
01:50:17:00
Avec l'aide d'Armando,

•

01:50:15:06
01:50:17:00
With the help of Armando,

•

01:50:17:04
01:50:19:18
un nouvel ami qui habitait Rome

•

01:50:17:04
01:50:19:18
a new friend from Rome

•

01:50:22:22
01:50:25:18
et que j'avais connu au festival,

•

01:50:22:22
01:50:25:18
I had met at the festival,

•

01:50:27:02
01:50:31:14
j'ai retrouvé la trace
de l'ami italien de mon père,

•

01:50:27:02
01:50:31:14
I was able to trace
my father's Italian friend,

•

01:50:32:04
01:50:33:06
Nino,

•

01:50:32:04
01:50:33:06
Nino,

•

01:50:34:02
01:50:36:16
qui lui avait raconté
l'histoire du vieux couple.

•

01:50:34:02
01:50:36:16
who had told him
the old couple's story.

	• 01:50:38:00 01:50:40:14
У него была греческая фамилия.	O apelido do Nino era de origem grega.
	• 01:50:41:14 01:50:45:02
Армандо посмотрел в телефонном справочнике.	O Armando procurou na lista telefónica.
	• 01:50:46:10 01:50:50:04
В Риме было только две семьи с такой фамилией,	Havia só dois com o mesmo nome em Roma,
	• 01:50:51:04 01:50:53:16
и первый номер, который он набрал,	e o primeiro a que ele ligou
	• 01:50:54:00 01:50:56:00
оказался верным.	era o certo.
	• 01:50:57:20 01:51:00:06
Нино умер много лет назад,	O Nino tinha morrido havia anos,

•

01:50:38:00
01:50:40:06
Il avait un nom grec.

•

01:50:41:14
01:50:45:02
Armando avait vérifié
dans l'annuaire.

•

01:50:46:10
01:50:50:04
Il y en avait deux à Rome,

•

01:50:51:04
01:50:53:16
et le premier qu'il a appelé

•

01:50:54:00
01:50:56:00
était le bon.

•

01:50:57:20
01:51:00:06
Nino était mort depuis
longtemps déjà,

•

01:50:38:00
01:50:40:06
He had a Greek surname.

•

01:50:41:14
01:50:45:02
Armando checked
the telephone book.

•

01:50:46:10
01:50:50:04
There were only two in Rome,

•

01:50:51:04
01:50:53:16
and the first he rang

•

01:50:54:00
01:50:56:00
was the right one.

•

01:50:57:20
01:51:00:06
Nino had died years ago,

•

01:51:01:12
01:51:05:16

но его жена и дочь по-прежнему жили по этому адресу.	mas a sua mulher e filha ainda viviam na mesma morada.

•

01:51:07:20
01:51:10:10

Армандо должен был возвращаться в Рим.	O Armando estava de regresso a Roma,

•

01:51:11:16
01:51:14:08

У меня было несколько свободных дней,	eu tinha ainda uns dias livres

•

01:51:14:20
01:51:17:04

и я решил поехать с ним.	e decidi ir com ele.

•

01:51:18:22
01:51:21:18

Мы говорили по-французски друг с другом,	Entre nós falávamos em francês,

•

01:51:22:20
01:51:25:10

но когда мы навещали семью Нино,	mas o Armando podia ser o meu tradutor

•

01:51:01:12
01:51:05:16
mais sa femme et sa fille
vivaient toujours à la même adresse.

•

01:51:01:12
01:51:05:16
but his wife and daughter
still lived at the same address.

•

01:51:07:20
01:51:10:10
Armando allait repartir
pour Rome,

•

01:51:07:20
01:51:10:10
Armando was going back to Rome,

•

01:51:11:16
01:51:14:08
j'avais quelques jours à perdre,

•

01:51:11:16
01:51:14:08
I had a few days to spare,

•

01:51:14:20
01:51:17:04
et j'ai décidé
de l'accompagner.

•

01:51:14:20
01:51:17:04
and I decided to go with him.

•

01:51:18:22
01:51:21:18
Entre nous,
nous parlions en français,

•

01:51:18:22
01:51:21:18
Between us we spoke French,

•

01:51:22:20
01:51:25:10
mais Armando pourrait
me servir d'interprète

•

01:51:22:20
01:51:25:10
but Armando would be my translator

•

01:51:25:20
01:51:29:04

Армандо пришлось быть моим переводчиком.	quando fôssemos visitar a família do Nino.

•

01:51:31:00
01:51:33:08

Дочь Нино звали Джина.	A filha do Nino chamava-se Gina.

•

01:51:34:14
01:51:36:14

А его жену - Вера.	Mas a sua mulher chamava-se Vera.

•

01:51:38:14
01:51:41:16

По-итальянски Вера значит «правдивая».	Em italiano, Vera significa «a verdadeira».

•

01:51:43:22
01:51:47:02

Если бы я придумал эту историю,	Tivesse-o eu inventado,

•

01:51:47:20
01:51:51:06

это было бы слабым местом в сценарии.	seria sinal de um guião mal escrito.

•

01:51:25:20
01:51:29:04
lors de notre rencontre
avec la famille de Nino.

•

01:51:25:20
01:51:29:04
when we went to visit Nino's family.

•

01:51:31:00
01:51:33:08
La fille de Nino
s'appelait Gina.

•

01:51:31:00
01:51:33:08
Nino's daughter was called Gina.

•

01:51:34:14
01:51:36:14
Mais sa femme
s'appelait Vera.

•

01:51:34:14
01:51:36:14
But Nino's wife was called Vera.

•

01:51:38:14
01:51:41:16
En italien,
Vera signifie «vraie».

•

01:51:38:14
01:51:41:16
In Italian,
Vera means "the truthful".

•

01:51:43:22
01:51:47:02
Si je l'avais inventé

•

01:51:43:22
01:51:47:02
Had I made it up

•

01:51:47:20
01:51:51:06
cela aurait été le signe
d'un script mal rédigé.

•

01:51:47:20
01:51:51:06
it would have been
bad scriptwriting.

•

01:51:52:20
01:51:56:14

Ведь именно она рассказала мне правду.	Viria a ser ela, ao fim de contas, quem me contaria a verdade.

•

01:51:58:06
01:51:59:18

С другой стороны,	Por outro lado,

•

01:52:00:10
01:52:02:14

голос за кадром - не мой.	esta não é a minha voz.

•

01:52:03:22
01:52:05:18

Это голос Юрия Степанова,	É a voz de Iúri Stepánov,

•

01:52:05:20
01:52:06:20

актёра.	um actor

•

01:52:07:18
01:52:11:10

Он говорит без характерного сибирского говора.	que não tem um sotaque siberiano.

•

01:51:52:20
01:51:55:20
Après tout, elle était celle
qui me dirait la vérité.

•

01:51:58:06
01:51:59:18
D'autre part,

•

01:52:00:10
01:52:02:14
ce n'est pas ma voix.

•

01:52:03:22
01:52:05:18
C'est celle de Youri Stepanov,

•

01:52:05:20
01:52:06:20
un acteur

•

01:52:07:18
01:52:11:10
qui n'a pas un accent
sibérien.

•

01:51:52:20
01:51:55:20
She was, after all,
the one who would tell me the truth.

•

01:51:58:06
01:51:59:18
On the other hand,

•

01:52:00:10
01:52:02:14
this is not my voice.

•

01:52:03:22
01:52:05:18
It's the voice of Yuri Stepanov,

•

01:52:05:20
01:52:06:20
an actor

•

01:52:07:18
01:52:11:10
who doesn't have
a Siberian accent.

•

01:52:12:08
01:52:14:00

Впрочем, я тоже.

Mas também eu não o tenho.

•

01:52:14:22
01:52:17:16

Я утратил его много лет назад.

Perdi-o há muito tempo.

•

01:52:22:20
01:52:26:12

Вера искренне рассмеялась, узнав,
зачем я пришёл.

A Vera riu-se a bom rir
do propósito da minha visita.

•

01:52:27:20
01:52:30:00

Я приехал из далёкой России,

Tinha eu vindo de tão longe,
da Rússia,

•

01:52:30:02
01:52:32:06

чтобы расспросить её

para lhe fazer perguntas

•

01:52:32:08
01:52:34:02

о стариках-мусорщиках?

sobre os velhos do lixo?

•

01:52:12:08
01:52:14:00
Moi non plus, d'ailleurs.

•

01:52:12:08
01:52:14:00
But neither do I.

•

01:52:14:22
01:52:17:16
Je l'ai perdu il y a longtemps.

•

01:52:14:22
01:52:17:16
I lost mine long ago.

•

01:52:22:20
01:52:26:12
Vera a ri de bon cœur
en apprenant le but de ma visite.

•

01:52:22:20
01:52:26:12
Vera laughed heartily
at the purpose of my visit.

•

01:52:27:20
01:52:30:00
Etais-je venu de si loin,
de Russie

•

01:52:27:20
01:52:30:00
Had I come all the way from Russia

•

01:52:30:02
01:52:32:06
pour lui poser des questions

•

01:52:30:02
01:52:33:12
to ask her about
the old couple of the rubbish?

•

01:52:32:08
01:52:34:02
sur l'histoire
du vieux couple aux ordures ?

•

01:52:36:00
01:52:38:18

Джина была слишком мала тогда
A Gina era na altura
ainda pequena demais

•

01:52:38:20
01:52:40:20

и ничего не помнила об этом.
para se lembrar deles.

•

01:52:42:16
01:52:45:06

Мы вчетвером сидели
вокруг стола, потягивая коньяк
Nós os quatro
com pequenos copos de conhaque

•

01:52:45:20
01:52:49:00

из маленьких рюмок.
à volta da mesa
da casa-de-jantar.

•

01:52:50:02
01:52:51:22

Я - в ожидании,
E eu à espera,

•

01:52:52:00
01:52:53:16

следя глазами
acompanhando com os olhos

•
01:52:36:00
01:52:38:02
Gina était trop jeune
à cette époque

•
01:52:36:00
01:52:40:16
Gina was too young then
to remember anything about them.

•
01:52:38:04
01:52:40:20
pour se rappeler quoi que ce soit
de cette histoire.

•
01:52:42:16
01:52:45:06
Nous quatre autour
de la table de la salle à manger,

•
01:52:42:16
01:52:49:00
The four of us with small glasses
of cognac around the dinning table.

•
01:52:45:20
01:52:49:00
avec des petits verres de cognac.

•
01:52:50:02
01:52:51:22
Et moi qui attendais,

•
01:52:50:02
01:52:50:24
And me waiting,

•
01:52:52:00
01:52:53:16
suivant des yeux
une conversation

•
01:52:51:02
01:52:56:24
following with my eyes a conversation
in a language I didn't understand.

•

01:52:53:18
01:52:56:24

за разговором
на непонятном языке.

uma conversa numa língua
que não compreendia.

•

01:52:58:20
01:52:59:22

Она сказала,

E então ela disse que,

•

01:53:00:06
01:53:01:18

что, во-первых,

para começar,

•

01:53:02:10
01:53:07:02

я был неправ, когда думал,
что они это делали вдвоём.

eu estava enganado
em pensar num casal.

•

01:53:08:12
01:53:11:06

Старуха одна

Tinha sido ela sozinha

•

01:53:11:20
01:53:14:22

таскала мусор
в свою квартиру на третьем этаже.

a acartar o lixo para
o apartamento do terceiro andar.

•

01:52:53:18
01:52:56:24
dans une langue
que je ne comprenais pas.

•

01:52:58:20
01:52:59:22
Alors elle a dit

•

01:52:58:20
01:52:59:22
And so she said,

•

01:53:00:06
01:53:01:18
que d'abord

•

01:53:00:06
01:53:01:18
that first of all

•

01:53:02:10
01:53:07:02
je me trompais
en pensant à un couple.

•

01:53:02:10
01:53:07:02
I was wrong in thinking
about a couple.

•

01:53:08:12
01:53:11:06
Seule la vieille femme

•

01:53:08:12
01:53:11:06
The old woman alone

•

01:53:11:20
01:53:14:22
avait transporté les ordures
dans l'appartement du troisième.

•

01:53:11:20
01:53:14:22
had dragged the rubbish up
to her third floor apartment.

	• 01:53:15:12 01:53:17:24
Только после смерти мужа.	Só depois da morte do marido.
	• 01:53:21:22 01:53:24:18
Я хотел проверить каждую деталь,	Eu queria certificar-me ponto por ponto
	• 01:53:25:20 01:53:28:08
всё, что я отчётливо помнил.	do que me lembrava claramente.
	• 01:53:29:16 01:53:35:10
Старик умер в больнице, после того, как его разбил паралич на улице.	O velho tinha morrido no hospital, depois dum ataque de coração na rua.
	• 01:53:36:20 01:53:40:02
Никаких лесов на доме не было.	Não tinha havido andaime algum.
	• 01:53:41:02 01:53:44:10
Никто даже не влезал через окно.	Ninguém tinha entrado pela janela.

•
01:53:15:12
01:53:17:24
Seulement après
la mort de son mari.

•
01:53:21:22
01:53:24:18
Je voulais vérifier
point par point

•
01:53:25:20
01:53:28:08
tout ce dont
je me souvenais clairement.

•
01:53:29:16
01:53:35:10
Le vieil homme était mort à l'hôpital
après une crise cardiaque dans la rue.

•
01:53:36:20
01:53:40:02
Il n'y avait jamais eu d'échafaudage.

•
01:53:41:02
01:53:44:10
Personne n'était passé
par une fenêtre.

•
01:53:15:12
01:53:17:24
Only after her husband had died.

•
01:53:21:22
01:53:24:18
I wanted to check
point by point

•
01:53:25:20
01:53:28:08
all I remembered clearly.

•
01:53:29:16
01:53:35:10
The old man had died in hospital
after a stroke in the street.

•
01:53:36:20
01:53:40:02
There was never any scaffolding.

•
01:53:41:02
01:53:44:10
No one
ever went in through a window.

•

01:53:45:08
01:53:48:14

Каждый раз власти взламывали дверь.	De cada uma das vezes as autoridades arrombaram a porta.

•

01:53:51:03
01:53:53:12

Она делала это трижды.	Ela fez aquilo três vezes.

•

01:53:54:04
01:53:56:20

Каждый раз мусор увозили,	De cada vez que levavam o lixo,

•

01:53:56:24
01:53:59:08

но она начинала опять.	ela recomeçava de novo.

•

01:54:00:10
01:54:02:22

Грузовик нагружали трижды,	Tinha havido três levas de camião,

•

01:53:45:08
01:53:46:10
A chaque visite,

•

01:53:45:08
01:53:48:12
Each time the authorities
had forced the door.

•

01:53:46:12
01:53:48:14
les autorités
avaient forcé la porte.

•

01:53:51:03
01:53:53:12
Elle avait recommencé trois fois.

•

01:53:51:03
01:53:53:12
She did it three times.

•

01:53:54:04
01:53:56:20
A chaque fois qu'on
emportait les ordures,

•

01:53:54:04
01:53:56:20
Each time
they took the rubbish away,

•

01:53:56:24
01:53:59:08
elle recommençait.

•

01:53:56:24
01:53:59:08
and each time
she would start again.

•

01:54:00:10
01:54:02:22
C'est lors de la première
visite uniquement

•

01:54:00:10
01:54:04:22
There were three truck loads,
but only on the first time.

	•
	01:54:03:00
	01:54:05:10
но только в первый раз.	mas só da primeira vez.
	•
	01:54:06:04
	01:54:09:14
После этого соседи действовали быстрее.	Os vizinhos aprenderam a actuar com mais rapidez.
	•
	01:54:12:00
	01:54:13:02
В конце концов	Por fim,
	•
	01:54:13:04
	01:54:15:20
её поместили в дом престарелых,	acabaram por levá-la para um lar de idosos,
	•
	01:54:16:14
	01:54:19:08
и она, должно быть, умерла там.	e provavelmente lá terá morrido.
	•
	01:54:20:22
	01:54:23:04
Вера точно не знала.	A Vera não tinha bem a certeza.

•

01:54:03:00
01:54:05:10
qu'il a fallu faire
trois chargements.

•

01:54:06:04
01:54:09:14
Les voisins avaient appris
à réagir plus vite.

•

01:54:06:04
01:54:09:14
The neighbours learned
to act faster.

•

01:54:12:00
01:54:13:02
A la fin,

•

01:54:12:00
01:54:13:02
In the end

•

01:54:13:04
01:54:15:20
elle a été placée
dans une maison de retraite

•

01:54:13:04
01:54:15:20
she was taken away
to an old people's home

•

01:54:16:14
01:54:19:08
et elle a dû y mourir.

•

01:54:16:14
01:54:19:08
and she must have died there.

•

01:54:20:22
01:54:23:04
Vera ne savait pas exactement.

•

01:54:20:22
01:54:23:04
Vera didn't know for sure.

	•
	01:54:25:06
	01:54:26:02
А также,	E não,

	•
	01:54:26:04
	01:54:28:04
ни старуха, ни её муж	nem a velha nem o seu marido

	•
	01:54:28:06
	01:54:30:02
не работали на почте.	tinham trabalhado nos correios.

	•
	01:54:30:20
	01:54:33:02
Они работали в булочной,	Tinham trabalhado numa padaria,

	•
	01:54:33:04
	01:54:35:08
разносили хлеб по домам.	vendendo pão ao domicílio.

	•
	01:54:39:22
Я хотел посмотреть	01:54:45:14
хотя бы на дом, если уж нельзя было увидеть квартиру.	Eu queria ver o prédio, mesmo que não visse o apartamento.

•
01:54:25:06
01:54:26:02
Et non,

•
01:54:25:06
01:54:26:02
And no,

•
01:54:26:04
01:54:28:04
ni la vieille femme
ni son mari

•
01:54:26:04
01:54:28:04
neither the old woman
nor her husband

•
01:54:28:06
01:54:30:02
n'avaient travaillé à la Poste.

•
01:54:28:06
01:54:30:02
had worked for the Post Office.

•
01:54:30:20
01:54:33:02
Ils avaient été employés
dans une boulangerie

•
01:54:30:20
01:54:32:18
They had worked for a bakery,

•
01:54:33:04
01:54:35:08
pour vendre du pain
à domicile.

•
01:54:32:20
01:54:35:02
selling bread door-to-door.

•
01:54:39:22
01:54:45:14
Je voulais voir le bâtiment,
à défaut de l'appartement.

•
01:54:39:22
01:54:45:14
I wanted to see the building,
if not the apartment.

•

01:54:47:04
01:54:50:14

Вера и Джина
вышли с нами на улицу.

A Vera e a Gina
desceram connosco até à rua.

•

01:54:51:14
01:54:55:08

Здание находилось через дом
от их жилья.

O prédio era o a seguir
ao prédio ao lado.

•

01:54:57:06
01:55:00:02

Вера указала на верхний этаж,

A Vera apontou
para o último andar,

•

01:55:03:16
01:55:06:20

где окно было наполовину открыто.

onde havia
uma janela entreaberta.

•

01:55:07:12
01:55:09:08

Кто живёт там теперь?

Quem vivia lá agora?

•

01:55:10:02
01:55:11:12

Никто.

Ninguém.

•
01:54:47:04
01:54:50:14
Vera et Gina sont descendues
avec nous dans la rue.

•
01:54:47:04
01:54:50:14
Vera and Gina
came down to the street with us.

•
01:54:51:14
01:54:55:08
Il s'agissait du second bâtiment
à partir du leur.

•
01:54:51:14
01:54:55:08
The building was the next
but one to theirs.

•
01:54:57:06
01:55:00:02
Vera a montré du doigt l'appartement
qui se trouvait au dernier étage,

•
01:54:57:06
01:55:00:02
Vera pointed to the top floor,

•
01:55:03:16
01:55:06:20
où une fenêtre était entrouverte.

•
01:55:03:16
01:55:06:20
where a window
had been left half-open.

•
01:55:07:12
01:55:09:08
Qui vivait là maintenant ?

•
01:55:07:12
01:55:09:08
Who lived there now?

•
01:55:10:02
01:55:11:12
Personne.

•
01:55:10:02
01:55:11:12
No one.

	• 01:55:12:22 01:55:17:00
Никто там не жил с тех пор, как старуха выехала.	Nunca mais lá tinha vivido alguém depois de a velha ter partido.
	• 01:55:18:20 01:55:22:06
Владелец был так огорчён происшедшим,	O que lá se tinha passado perturbou tanto o senhorio
	• 01:55:22:16 01:55:27:04
что одно время вообще не хотел снова сдавать эту квартиру.	que, na altura, não quis voltar a alugá-lo.
	• 01:55:29:00 01:55:30:18
Шли годы,	Depressa se passaram anos,
	• 01:55:30:20 01:55:33:18
квартира становилась всё более запущенной,	o apartamento degradou-se,
	• 01:55:34:21 01:55:37:04
там поселились голуби,	os pombos entraram lá para dentro.

•

01:55:12:22
01:55:17:00
Personne n'y avait jamais plus vécu
après le départ de la vieille femme.

•

01:55:18:20
01:55:22:06
Le propriétaire avait été tellement
perturbé par ce qui s'était passé

•

01:55:22:16
01:55:27:04
qu'il n'avait pas voulu
le relouer.

•

01:55:29:00
01:55:30:18
Les années ont passé si vite,

•

01:55:30:20
01:55:33:18
l'appartement s'est délabré,

•

01:55:34:21
01:55:37:04
les pigeons y sont entrés.

•

01:55:12:22
01:55:17:00
No one had ever lived there
after the old woman left.

•

01:55:18:20
01:55:22:06
The landlord had been
so disturbed by what had happened

•

01:55:22:16
01:55:27:04
that at the time he hadn't wanted
to let it out again.

•

01:55:29:00
01:55:30:18
Soon years had passed,

•

01:55:30:20
01:55:33:18
it fell into disrepair,

•

01:55:34:21
01:55:37:04
pigeons got in.

	• 01:55:37:06 01:55:39:06
владелец состарился.	O senhorio era velho.
	• 01:55:40:12 01:55:43:04
Соседи по-прежнему жаловались,	Os vizinhos ainda se queixavam,
	• 01:55:43:18 01:55:46:22
на сей раз на непрерывное воркование голубей,	agora do arrulhar incessante dos pombos
	• 01:55:46:24 01:55:48:18
которые много лет жили там	que há anos lá viviam
	• 01:55:48:20 01:55:50:20
и высиживали птенцов.	e faziam criação.
	• 01:55:52:20 01:55:56:06
Я не видел снующих туда-сюда голубей,	Não vi pombos nenhuns a entrar e a sair,

•
01:55:37:06
01:55:39:06
Le propriétaire était âgé.

•
01:55:37:06
01:55:39:06
The landlord was old.

•
01:55:40:12
01:55:42:24
Les voisins se plaignaient toujours,

•
01:55:40:12
01:55:42:24
The neighbours still complained,

•
01:55:43:18
01:55:45:20
maintenant, du roucoulement
incessant des pigeons

•
01:55:43:18
01:55:45:20
now about the incessant cooing
of the pigeons

•
01:55:45:22
01:55:47:02
qui depuis des années

•
01:55:45:22
01:55:48:20
who had lived and bred there

•
01:55:47:04
01:55:50:20
nichaient et se reproduisaient
dans l'appartement.

•
01:55:48:22
01:55:50:20
for years.

•
01:55:52:20
01:55:56:06
Je n'ai pas vu
de pigeon entrer et sortir,

•
01:55:52:20
01:55:56:06
I saw no pigeons going in and out,

	• 01:55:56:08 01:56:00:00
но Вера и Джина уверяли меня,	mas a Vera e a Gina garantiram-me que sim,
	• 01:56:00:02 01:56:01:22
что они делают это всё время,	que o faziam a toda a hora,
	• 01:56:02:08 01:56:04:16
все дни напролёт.	o dia inteiro.
	• 01:56:06:12 01:56:09:04
У меня с собой был фотоаппарат,	Tinha comigo uma máquina fotográfica,
	• 01:56:10:00 01:56:12:10
но я не хотел фотографировать.	mas não quis tirar fotografias.
	• 01:56:17:10 01:56:20:12
Был яркий, ослепительный день.	Era um dia de sol, de uma luz de cegar.

•
01:55:56:08
01:56:00:00
mais Vera et Gina
m'ont assuré que c'était bien le cas,

•
01:55:56:08
01:56:00:00
but Vera and Gina
assured me that they did,

•
01:56:00:02
01:56:01:22
constamment,

•
01:56:00:02
01:56:01:22
all the time,

•
01:56:02:08
01:56:04:16
à longueur de journée.

•
01:56:02:08
01:56:04:16
all day long.

•
01:56:06:12
01:56:09:04
J'avais un appareil photo avec moi

•
01:56:06:12
01:56:09:04
I had a camera with me

•
01:56:10:00
01:56:12:10
mais je n'ai pas voulu m'en servir.

•
01:56:10:00
01:56:12:10
but I didn't want to take photographs.

•
01:56:17:10
01:56:20:12
C'était une journée ensoleillée,
d'une lumière aveuglante.

•
01:56:17:10
01:56:19:20
It was a bright, blinding day.

	•
	01:56:21:00
	01:56:24:22
Ничего общего с тем, как я представлял себе Рим.	Nada se parecia com o que eu tinha imaginado de Roma.
	•
	01:56:28:04
	01:56:30:22
Я испытывал острую тоску.	Senti-me augustiado e triste.
	•
	01:56:31:12
	01:56:34:06
Со мной случилось что-то ужасное,	Tinha-me acontecido qualquer coisa de horrível,
	•
	01:56:34:08
	01:56:36:02
там, на тротуаре,	ali, no passeio,
	•
	01:56:36:04
	01:56:39:22
где стояли Армандо, Джина и Вера.	com o Armando, a Gina e a Vera.
	•
	01:56:40:12
	01:56:43:04
Я не хотел, чтобы они заметили.	E não quis que dessem por isso.

•
01:56:21:00
01:56:24:22
Rien à Rome ne ressemblait
à ce que j'avais imaginé.

•
01:56:21:00
01:56:24:22
Nothing resembled
what I had imagined of Rome.

•
01:56:28:04
01:56:30:22
Je me suis senti
angoissé et triste.

•
01:56:28:04
01:56:30:22
I felt anguished and sad.

•
01:56:31:12
01:56:34:06
Quelque chose de terrible
m'était arrivé,

•
01:56:31:12
01:56:34:06
Something terrible
had happened to me,

•
01:56:34:08
01:56:36:02
là, sur le trottoir

•
01:56:34:08
01:56:36:02
there on the pavement

•
01:56:36:04
01:56:39:22
avec Armando, Gina, et Vera.

•
01:56:36:04
01:56:39:22
with Armando, and Gina, and Vera.

•
01:56:40:12
01:56:43:04
Et je ne voulais pas le montrer.

•
01:56:40:12
01:56:43:04
And I didn't want it to show.

	• 01:56:47:22 01:56:50:02
Я был не в том фильме.	Estava no filme errado.
	• 01:56:55:08 01:56:57:12
Кто изменил историю?	Quem tinha mudado a história?
	• 01:56:57:16 01:56:58:16
Нино?	O Nino?
	• 01:56:59:10 01:57:00:16
Мой отец?	O meu pai?
	• 01:57:01:12 01:57:02:12
Вера?	A Vera?
	• 01:57:04:16 01:57:06:22
Мой отец не был лгуном	O meu pai não era mentiroso,

•
01:56:47:22
01:56:50:02
Je n'étais pas dans le bon film.

•
01:56:47:22
01:56:50:02
I was in the wrong film.

•
01:56:55:08
01:56:57:12
Qui avait changé l'histoire ?

•
01:56:55:08
01:56:57:12
Who had changed the story?

•
01:56:57:16
01:56:58:16
Nino ?

•
01:56:57:16
01:56:58:16
Nino?

•
01:56:59:10
01:57:00:16
Mon père ?

•
01:56:59:10
01:57:00:16
My father?

•
01:57:01:12
01:57:02:12
Vera ?

•
01:57:01:12
01:57:02:12
Vera?

•
01:57:04:16
01:57:06:22
Mon père n'était pas menteur,

•
01:57:04:18
01:57:09:06
My father wasn't a liar,
nor a very imaginative man.

•

01:57:06:24
01:57:09:12

и не отличался богатым
воображением.

nem um homem
muito imaginativo.

•

01:57:11:00
01:57:14:24

Нино... Я ничего не знал о нём.

O Nino, eu não sabia nada
acerca dele.

•

01:57:15:18
01:57:18:14

Я видел его фото, в рамке

Vi a sua fotografia,
emoldurada,

•

01:57:18:20
01:57:21:22

на стене в столовой у Веры.

na parede
da casa-de-jantar da Vera.

•

01:57:23:18
01:57:25:24

Он выглядел безлико,

Tinha o ar anónimo

•

01:57:26:00
01:57:28:02

как все покойные мужья

de todos os maridos defuntos

•
01:57:06:24
01:57:09:12
ni quelqu'un
de très imaginatif non plus.

•
01:57:11:00
01:57:14:24
Nino,
je ne savais rien de lui.

•
01:57:11:00
01:57:14:24
Nino, I knew nothing about him.

•
01:57:15:18
01:57:18:14
J'ai vu sa photo,
encadrée,

•
01:57:15:18
01:57:18:14
I saw his photograph, framed,

•
01:57:18:20
01:57:21:22
sur le mur de la salle à manger
de Vera.

•
01:57:18:20
01:57:21:22
on Vera's dining room wall.

•
01:57:23:18
01:57:25:24
Il paraissait aussi anonyme

•
01:57:23:18
01:57:25:24
He looked as anonymous

•
01:57:26:00
01:57:28:02
que tous les maris décédés

•
01:57:26:00
01:57:28:02
as all the dead husbands

	• 01:57:28:04 01:57:29:24
на чёрно-белых фото.	a preto e branco.
	• 01:57:37:00 01:57:39:12
О Вере я тоже ничего не знал,	Também não sabia nada sobre a Vera,
	• 01:57:39:14 01:57:41:14
но я ей верил.	mas acreditava nela.
	• 01:57:46:11 01:57:48:08
Мы вышли поужинать в тот вечер,	Nessa noite fomos jantar fora,
	• 01:57:48:10 01:57:50:06
Армандо и я.	o Armando e eu.
	• 01:57:51:00 01:57:52:20
Я был неразговорчив.	Não me apetecia falar.

•
01:57:28:04
01:57:29:24
en noir et blanc.

•
01:57:28:04
01:57:29:24
in black and white.

•
01:57:37:00
01:57:39:12
Je ne savais rien
de Vera non plus,

•
01:57:37:00
01:57:39:12
I also didn't know
anything about Vera,

•
01:57:39:14
01:57:41:14
mais je la croyais.

•
01:57:39:14
01:57:41:14
but I believed her.

•
01:57:46:11
01:57:48:08
Nous sommes sortis dîner
ce soir-là,

•
01:57:46:11
01:57:48:08
We went out for dinner that evening,

•
01:57:48:10
01:57:50:06
Armando et moi.

•
01:57:48:10
01:57:50:06
Armando and I.

•
01:57:51:00
01:57:52:20
Je n'avais pas
trop envie de parler.

•
01:57:51:00
01:57:52:20
I wasn't talking much.

	• 01:57:54:08 01:57:56:10
Армандо сказал то,	Foi o Armando quem o disse.
	• 01:57:56:12 01:57:58:08
что я уже знал.	O que eu já sabia.
	• 01:57:58:16 01:58:00:14
Почему я не включил себя	Por que não me tinha eu incluído
	• 01:58:00:16 01:58:02:20
в список подозреваемых?	na lista dos suspeitos?
	• 01:58:03:14 01:58:05:20
Скорее всего, это я	Eu era de todos o mais susceptível
	• 01:58:05:22 01:58:08:12
хотел, чтобы жизнь была похожа на фильм.	de querer que a vida se parecesse com um filme.

•
01:57:54:08
01:57:56:10
C'est Armando qui l'a dit.

•
01:57:56:12
01:57:58:08
Ce que je savais déjà.

•
01:57:58:16
01:58:00:14
Pourquoi ne m'étais-je pas inclus

•
01:58:00:16
01:58:02:20
dans la liste des suspects ?

•
01:58:03:14
01:58:05:20
J'étais celui
qui était le plus susceptible

•
01:58:05:22
01:58:08:12
de vouloir que la vie
ressemble à un film.

•
01:57:54:08
01:57:56:10
It was Armando who said it.

•
01:57:56:12
01:57:58:08
What I already knew.

•
01:57:58:16
01:58:00:14
Why had I not included myself

•
01:58:00:16
01:58:02:20
in the list of suspects?

•
01:58:03:14
01:58:05:20
I was the one most likely

•
01:58:05:22
01:58:08:12
to want life to resemble a film.

•

01:58:10:10
01:58:12:08

Мы допоздна говорили,

Falámos até tarde

•

01:58:12:10
01:58:14:00

сидя на ресторанной террасе,

na esplanada
de um restaurante

•

01:58:14:10
01:58:18:08

украшенной гирляндами
разноцветных лампочек.

iluminada por séries
de lâmpadas coloridas.

•

01:58:19:06
01:58:21:06

Это был Рим.

Era Roma.

•

01:58:22:10
01:58:24:00

Римский фильм,

Um filme romano

•

01:58:24:02
01:58:27:18

в котором я разговариваю
с Армандо,

em que eu falava
com o Armando

•
01:58:10:10
01:58:12:08
Nous avons discuté
tard dans la nuit

•
01:58:10:10
01:58:12:08
We talked until late

•
01:58:12:10
01:58:14:00
à la terrasse d'un restaurant

•
01:58:12:10
01:58:14:00
on the terrace of a restaurant

•
01:58:14:10
01:58:18:08
au-dessus de laquelle pendaient
des ampoules multicolores.

•
01:58:14:10
01:58:18:08
with strings of coloured light bulbs.

•
01:58:19:06
01:58:21:06
C'était Rome.

•
01:58:19:06
01:58:21:06
It was Rome.

•
01:58:22:10
01:58:24:00
Un film romain

•
01:58:22:10
01:58:24:00
A Roman film

•
01:58:24:02
01:58:27:18
dans lequel
je parlais avec Armando

•
01:58:24:02
01:58:27:18
where I talked to Armando

•

01:58:28:18
01:58:31:06

так же, как говорил с Петром.

como tinha falado
com o Pïotr.

•

01:58:32:10
01:58:34:00

О воспоминаниях.

Sobre memórias.

•

01:58:36:16
01:58:41:10

На этот раз я был в шоке
из-за уничтоженного сценария,

Desta vez eu estava debaixo
do choque de ver um guião destruído.

•

01:58:42:06
01:58:44:20

и у меня не было
ни уверенности в себе,

E não tive nem a vontade,

•

01:58:45:16
01:58:49:10

ни желания
играть роль перед ним.

nem a confiança em mim
de representar para ele.

•

01:58:28:18
01:58:31:06
comme j'avais parlé
avec Piotr.

•

01:58:28:18
01:58:31:06
as I had talked to Piotr.

•

01:58:32:10
01:58:34:00
De souvenirs.

•

01:58:32:10
01:58:34:00
About memories.

•

01:58:36:16
01:58:41:10
Cette fois, j'étais sous le choc
de voir détruit un scénario.

•

01:58:36:16
01:58:41:10
This time I was under the shock
of a wiped out scenario.

•

01:58:42:06
01:58:44:20
Et je n'ai pas eu le désir

•

01:58:42:06
01:58:44:20
And I didn't have the desire,

•

01:58:45:16
01:58:49:10
ni l'assurance nécessaires
pour jouer pour lui.

•

01:58:45:16
01:58:46:10
nor confidence,

•

01:58:46:12
01:58:49:04
to perform for him.

	• 01:58:50:16 01:58:52:08
Я сказал Армандо,	Disse ao Armando
	• 01:58:52:10 01:58:55:24
что хочу опять пойти к дому на следующий день	que queria voltar ao prédio no dia seguinte,
	• 01:58:56:08 01:58:59:02
и дождаться вылетающих голубей.	e esperar para ver os pombos.
	• 01:59:00:08 01:59:02:00
Но Армандо сказал:	E o Armando disse:
	• 01:59:02:02 01:59:03:10
«Не надо.	«Não vás.
	• 01:59:04:20 01:59:06:20
Это Верина история.	Essa é a história da Vera.

•
01:58:50:16
01:58:52:08
J'ai dit à Armando

•
01:58:50:16
01:58:52:08
I told Armando

•
01:58:52:10
01:58:55:24
que je voulais retourner
près du bâtiment le lendemain

•
01:58:52:10
01:58:55:24
I wanted to go back to the building
the following day

•
01:58:56:08
01:58:59:02
et attendre
de voir les pigeons.

•
01:58:56:08
01:58:59:02
and wait to see the pigeons.

•
01:59:00:08
01:59:02:00
Armando m'a dit :

•
01:59:00:08
01:59:02:00
And Armando said:

•
01:59:02:02
01:59:03:10
«N'y va pas.

•
01:59:02:02
01:59:03:10
"Don't.

•
01:59:04:20
01:59:06:20
Ça, c'est l'histoire de Vera.

•
01:59:04:20
01:59:06:20
That's Vera's story.

•

01:59:08:20
01:59:10:10

А не твоя.»

Não a tua.»

•

01:59:15:04
01:59:16:24

Мне было одиноко.

Senti-me sozinho.

•

01:59:17:20
01:59:19:18

Я тосковал по жене,

Quis ter a minha mulher

•

01:59:19:20
01:59:22:14

хотел, чтобы она лежала рядом.

deitada ao meu lado.

•

01:59:23:04
01:59:26:22

Хотел почувствовать её локоть
рядом с моим.

O cotovelo dela
dentro do meu.

•

01:59:28:14
01:59:32:10

Но её не будет
в моей гостиничной кровати.

Ela não estaria
na minha cama de hotel.

•

01:59:08:20
01:59:10:10
Pas la tienne.»

•

01:59:08:20
01:59:10:10
Not yours.“

•

01:59:15:04
01:59:16:24
Je me suis senti seul.

•

01:59:15:04
01:59:16:24
I felt lonely.

•

01:59:17:20
01:59:19:18
Desireux d'avoir ma femme

•

01:59:17:20
01:59:19:18
Longed for my wife

•

01:59:19:20
01:59:22:14
allongée à mes côtés.

•

01:59:19:20
01:59:22:14
lying beside me.

•

01:59:23:04
01:59:26:22
Son coude
dans le creux de mon bras.

•

01:59:23:04
01:59:26:22
Her elbow inside the hollow of mine.

•

01:59:28:14
01:59:32:10
Elle ne serait pas
dans mon lit d'hôtel.

•

01:59:28:14
01:59:32:10
She wouldn't be in my hotel bed.

	• 01:59:37:20 01:59:42:12
Я продолжал думать о голубях, снующих туда-сюда.	Os pombos continuavam a entrar e sair da minha cabeça.
	• 01:59:44:18 01:59:46:20
В ту ночь у меня было видение	Nessa noite, no escuro do meu quarto,
	• 01:59:46:22 01:59:49:08
в темноте моей комнаты.	tive uma visão.
	• 01:59:50:16 01:59:52:10
Пол квартиры,	O chão daquele apartamento
	• 01:59:52:12 01:59:56:04
покрытый многолетним голубиным помётом.	coberto de caca de pombo de muitos anos.
	• 01:59:56:20 01:59:58:10
Серо-белая жижа	Uma pasta cinzenta e branca.

•

01:59:37:20
01:59:42:12
Ces pigeons continuaient
à entrer et sortir de ma tête.

•

01:59:37:20
01:59:42:12
Those pigeons kept flying
in and out of my head.

•

01:59:44:18
01:59:46:20
Cette nuit-là,
j'ai eu une vision

•

01:59:44:18
01:59:46:20
That night I had a vision

•

01:59:46:22
01:59:49:08
dans l'obscurité de ma chambre.

•

01:59:46:22
01:59:49:08
in the darkness of my room.

•

01:59:50:16
01:59:52:10
Le sol de cet appartement

•

01:59:50:16
01:59:52:10
That apartment's floor

•

01:59:52:12
01:59:56:04
recouvert de la fiente de pigeon
de tant d'années.

•

01:59:52:12
01:59:56:04
covered in the pigeon shit
of many years.

•

01:59:56:20
01:59:58:10
Une pâte grise et blanche.

•

01:59:56:20
01:59:58:10
A grey and white paste.

•

01:59:58:12
02:00:00:12

цвета чернил на снегу.

Da cor de tinta
sobre a neve.

•

02:00:06:14
02:00:09:16

И как всегда,
Байкал явился мне.

E, como de costume,
o Baikal veio ter comigo.

•

02:00:10:12
02:00:13:06

Как музыка являлась моей маме.

Como a música
tinha ido ter com a minha mãe.

•

02:00:15:06
02:00:17:20

Воспоминания о его звуках

E a memória
dos sons do Baikal

•

02:00:17:22
02:00:21:06

нашептывали птичьи песни
и крики,

murmurou-me cantos
e gritos de pássaros,

•

02:00:22:02
02:00:25:10

его волны плескались, лаская слух,

e as suas ondas
bateram-me ao ouvido

•

01:59:58:12
02:00:00:12
De la couleur de l'encre
sur la neige.

•

01:59:58:12
02:00:00:12
The colour of ink on snow.

•

02:00:06:14
02:00:09:16
Et comme d'habitude,
le Baïkal m'est revenu.

•

02:00:06:16
02:00:09:16
And as usual,
the Baikal came to me.

•

02:00:10:12
02:00:13:06
De la même façon que
la musique revenait à ma mère.

•

02:00:10:14
02:00:13:06
As music had come to my mother.

•

02:00:15:06
02:00:17:20
Et le souvenir de ses sons

•

02:00:15:06
02:00:17:20
And the memory of its sounds

•

02:00:17:22
02:00:21:06
m'a murmuré des chants
et des cris d'oiseaux,

•

02:00:17:22
02:00:21:06
whispered birds' songs
and cries,

•

02:00:22:02
02:00:25:20
et ses vagues ont clapoté

•

02:00:22:02
02:00:25:20
and its waves lapped against my ear

•

02:00:25:20
02:00:27:18

убаюкивая меня, | e embalaram-me

•

02:00:27:20
02:00:29:08

и я уснул. | até adormecer.

•

02:00:32:00
02:00:34:02

За ужином я сказал Армандо, | Ao jantar
eu tinha contado ao Armando

•

02:00:34:04
02:00:35:18

что буряты | que a gente da Buriátia

•

02:00:35:20
02:00:39:02

плещут молоком в лебедей,
приветствуя их. | ainda atira leite aos cisnes
num gesto de boas-vindas.

•

02:00:40:04
02:00:42:24

Они верят, что произошли от
лебедей. | Acreditam que são
seus descendentes.

•
02:00:25:22
02:00:27:16
contre mes oreilles

•
02:00:28:00
02:00:29:08
et m'ont bercé.

•
02:00:32:00
02:00:34:02
Au dîner,
j'avais dit à Armando

•
02:00:34:04
02:00:35:18
que les bouryats

•
02:00:35:20
02:00:39:02
jettent encore du lait aux cygnes
pour leur souhaiter la bienvenue.

•
02:00:40:04
02:00:42:24
Ils croient en être les descendants.

•
02:00:25:22
02:00:29:08
and rocked me to sleep.

•
02:00:32:00
02:00:34:02
At dinner I had told Armando

•
02:00:34:04
02:00:35:18
that the Buryat people

•
02:00:35:20
02:00:39:02
still throw milk at swans
as a welcoming gesture.

•
02:00:40:04
02:00:42:24
They believe
they are descended from them.

	• 02:00:44:02 02:00:48:06
В одной из их сказок говорится о молодом парне, Хоридо,	Uma das suas histórias é a de um jovem, Khorido,
	• 02:00:48:22 02:00:51:06
сыне шаманки Исыхем.	filho de uma mulher xamã, Issikhem.
	• 02:00:52:18 02:00:57:04
Исыхем была бездетна и очень хотела иметь детей.	Issikhem não tinha filhos e queria muito tê-los.
	• 02:00:58:20 02:01:01:00
Она попросила богов Байкала	Pediu ao deuses do Baikal
	• 02:01:01:02 02:01:04:06
принести трёх мальчиков на берег.	que fizessem aparecer três meninos na praia,
	• 02:01:05:14 02:01:07:20
Боги сделали это для неё.	e assim fizeram.

•

02:00:44:02
02:00:48:06
L'une de leurs légendes
est celle du jeune Khorido,

•

02:00:48:22
02:00:51:06
le fils d'une shaman appelée
Isykhem.

•

02:00:52:18
02:00:57:04
Isykhem n'avait pas d'enfant
et en voulait désespérément.

•

02:00:58:20
02:01:01:00
Alors elle a demandé
aux dieux du Baïkal

•

02:01:01:02
02:01:04:06
de faire apparaître
trois nouveau-nés mâles sur la rive,

•

02:01:05:14
02:01:07:20
ce qu'ils ont fait.

•

02:00:44:02
02:00:48:06
One of their tales is of a young man,
Khorido,

•

02:00:48:22
02:00:51:06
the son of a shaman woman,
Isykhem.

•

02:00:52:18
02:00:57:04
Isykhem had no children
and longed for them.

•

02:00:58:20
02:01:01:00
She asked the gods of the Baikal

•

02:01:01:02
02:01:03:22
to cast three baby boys
on the shore,

•

02:01:05:14
02:01:07:20
and they did.

	• 02:01:08:12 02:01:10:16
Мальчиков звали Ахирит,	Eram eles Akhirit,
	• 02:01:11:10 02:01:12:06
Былагат	Bilagat,
	• 02:01:12:08 02:01:13:21
и Хоридо.	e Khorido.
	• 02:01:14:10 02:01:17:16
Они выросли храбрыми охотниками.	Cresceram e tornaram-se valentes caçadores.
	• 02:01:18:18 02:01:20:24
Однажды Ахирит и Былагат	Um dia, Ahkirit e Bilagat
	• 02:01:21:02 02:01:22:22
обидели Хоридо,	foram injustos para com Khorido,

•
02:01:08:12
02:01:10:16
Ils se prénommaient Akhirit,

•
02:01:08:12
02:01:10:16
They were Akhirit,

•
02:01:11:10
02:01:12:06
Bylagat,

•
02:01:11:10
02:01:12:06
Bylagat,

•
02:01:12:08
02:01:13:21
et Khorido.

•
02:01:12:08
02:01:13:21
and Khorido.

•
02:01:14:10
02:01:17:16
Ils ont grandi et sont devenus
de valeureux chasseurs.

•
02:01:14:10
02:01:17:16
They grew to be brave hunters.

•
02:01:18:18
02:01:21:14
Un jour qu'ils se partageaient
le fruit de leur chasse

•
02:01:18:20
02:01:21:00
One day Akhirit and Bylagat

•
02:01:21:16
02:01:22:22
Akhirit et Bylagat

•
02:01:21:02
02:01:22:16
were unfair to Khorido

•

02:01:22:24
02:01:26:02

когда делили
добычу после охоты.

ao dividir
os espolios da caça,

•

02:01:27:22
02:01:30:20

Хоридо отправился
к берегам Байкала.

e Khorido partiu em direcção
às margens do Baikal.

•

02:01:31:14
02:01:34:20

Он увидел лебедей, садящихся
на воду.

Viu cisnes
aterrando na água,

•

02:01:35:00
02:01:39:08

Коснувшись воды,
они превратились
в прекрасных девушек.

que ao tocá-la transformavam-se
em belas donzelas.

•

02:01:40:20
02:01:44:06

Он спрятал оперение
самой красивой девушки,

Khorido escondeu as penas
da mais bela de todas,

•

02:01:45:06
02:01:47:12

и когда она вышла из воды,

de modo que
quando ela saísse da água

•
02:01:22:24
02:01:26:06
ont été injustes
envers Khorido,

•
02:01:27:22
02:01:30:20
et il est parti
vers les rives du Baïkal.

•
02:01:31:14
02:01:34:20
Là, il a vu des cygnes qui,
dès qu'ils se posaient sur l'eau,

•
02:01:35:00
02:01:39:08
se transformaient
en belles jeunes filles.

•
02:01:40:20
02:01:44:06
Il a caché les plumes
de la plus belle d'entre elles

•
02:01:45:06
02:01:47:12
pour l'empêcher de repartir

•
02:01:22:22
02:01:26:06
when dividing
the spoils of their hunt,

•
02:01:27:22
02:01:30:20
and Khorido set off
to the shores of the Baikal.

•
02:01:31:16
02:01:34:10
He saw swans landing on the water,

•
02:01:35:00
02:01:39:12
and when they touched it
they turned into beautiful maidens.

•
02:01:40:20
02:01:44:06
He hid the feathers
of the most beautiful maiden,

•
02:01:45:06
02:01:47:12
so that when she came out
of the water

•
02:01:47:14
02:01:49:18

она не могла улететь.	não pudesse partir voando.

•
02:01:50:16
02:01:53:06

Horидо отказался вернуть её перья	Recusou-se a entregar-lhe as penas,

•
02:01:53:08
02:01:55:16

и предложил жениться на ней.	e em vez disso propôs-lhe casamento.

•
02:01:56:10
02:01:58:00

Она согласилась.	Ela aceitou.

•
02:02:00:00
02:02:05:00

Они счастливо стали жить в юрте, и у них родилось 11 детей.	Viveram felizes numa tenda de peles e tiveram 11 filhos.

•
02:02:06:02
02:02:08:12

Когда она состарилась,	Quando ela já era muito velha,

•
02:01:47:14
02:01:49:18
lorsqu'elle sortirait de l'eau.

•
02:01:47:14
02:01:49:18
she couldn't fly away.

•
02:01:50:16
02:01:53:06
Il a refusé
de lui redonner ses plumes,

•
02:01:50:16
02:01:55:16
He refused to return her feathers,
and instead offered to marry her.

•
02:01:53:08
02:01:55:16
et lui a proposé de l'épouser.

•
02:01:56:10
02:01:58:00
Elle a accepté.

•
02:01:56:10
02:01:58:00
She accepted.

•
02:02:00:00
02:02:05:00
Ils ont vécu heureux dans une yourte
et ont eu 11 enfants.

•
02:02:00:00
02:02:05:00
They lived happily in a yurt
and had 11 children.

•
02:02:06:02
02:02:08:12
Devenue vieille,

•
02:02:06:02
02:02:08:12
When she became an old woman,

•

02:02:08:14
02:02:11:00

она снова попросила
вернуть ей оперение.

pediu novamente a Khorido
que lhe devolvesse as penas.

•

02:02:12:04
02:02:14:06

Хоридо исполнил её желание.

Khorido cumpriu
o seu desejo,

•

02:02:14:08
02:02:17:18

Он думал, что прожив на земле
так долго,

crendo que
depois de tanto tempo na terra

•

02:02:18:00
02:02:20:06

она не захочет убежать.

ela não quereria fugir.

•

02:02:21:14
02:02:23:16

Однако, получив оперение,

Mas assim que as recebeu

•

02:02:23:18
02:02:26:20

она сразу выпорхнула из юрты.

levantou voo,
abandonando a tenda.

•
02:02:08:14
02:02:10:18
elle l'a prié
de lui rendre ses plumes.

•
02:02:08:14
02:02:10:18
she again requested
her feathers be returned to her.

•
02:02:12:04
02:02:14:06
Khorido a exaucé son vœu,

•
02:02:12:04
02:02:17:18
Khorido complied with her wish,
believing that after so long on earth

•
02:02:14:08
02:02:17:18
croyant qu'après
tant de temps sur terre

•
02:02:18:00
02:02:20:06
elle ne voudrait pas s'échapper.

•
02:02:18:00
02:02:20:06
she wouldn't want to escape.

•
02:02:21:14
02:02:23:16
Mais dès qu'il les lui a redonné,

•
02:02:21:14
02:02:26:20
However, as soon as this was done
she flew out of the yurt.

•
02:02:23:18
02:02:26:20
elle a pris son envol
et est partie de la yourte.

	• 02:02:33:10 02:02:34:14
В школе я узнал,	Na escola, aprendi
	• 02:02:34:16 02:02:38:14
что в Байкал впадает 336 рек,	que 336 rios correm para o Baikal
	• 02:02:38:18 02:02:41:14
и только одна вытекает из него:	e que apenas um corre para fora dele:
	• 02:02:41:20 02:02:42:24
Ангара.	o Angara.
	• 02:02:44:22 02:02:47:12
Говорят, в Новосибирске жил мальчик,	Parece que havia um rapaz da escola, em Novossibirsk,
	• 02:02:47:14 02:02:51:08
который наизусть знал названия всех этих рек,	que conseguia recitar de cor os nomes de todos os rios,

•

02:02:33:10
02:02:34:14
J'ai appris à l'école

•

02:02:33:10
02:02:34:14
I learned in school

•

02:02:34:16
02:02:38:14
que 336 rivières se jettent
dans le Baïkal,

•

02:02:34:16
02:02:38:14
that 336 rivers flow into the Baikal,

•

02:02:38:18
02:02:41:14
et qu'une seule en sort :

•

02:02:38:18
02:02:41:14
and only one flows out of it:

•

02:02:41:20
02:02:42:24
l'Angara.

•

02:02:41:20
02:02:42:24
the Angara.

•

02:02:44:22
02:02:47:12
Apparemment,
il y avait un écolier à Novosibirsk

•

02:02:44:22
02:02:47:12
Apparently there was a schoolboy
in Novosibirsk

•

02:02:47:14
02:02:51:08
qui pouvait réciter
tous leurs noms par cœur,

•

02:02:47:14
02:02:51:08
who could recite by heart
all their names

•

02:02:51:12
02:02:53:06

не в алфавитном порядке,

não por ordem alfabética

•

02:02:53:22
02:02:56:24

а по кругу,
как это видно на карте.

mas num círculo,
tal como no mapa.

•

02:02:57:02
02:02:59:06

От Ангары на север,

Do Angara
em direcção ao norte,

•

02:02:59:10
02:03:00:20

потом на юг

depois para sul,

•

02:03:01:00
02:03:02:20

и опять к Ангаре.

e de volta ao Angara.

•

02:03:05:18
02:03:08:10

Я никогда не пытался запомнить их.

Eu nunca tentei.

•
02:02:51:12
02:02:53:06
pas par ordre alphabétique

•
02:02:51:12
02:02:53:06
not in alphabetical order

•
02:02:53:22
02:02:56:24
mais telles qu'elles étaient dessinées sur la carte.

•
02:02:53:22
02:02:56:24
but in a circle, as mapped.

•
02:02:57:02
02:02:59:06
De l'Angara vers le nord,

•
02:02:57:02
02:02:59:06
From the Angara to the north,

•
02:02:59:10
02:03:00:20
puis au sud,

•
02:02:59:10
02:03:00:20
then south,

•
02:03:01:00
02:03:02:20
et de là jusqu'à l'Angara.

•
02:03:01:00
02:03:02:20
and back to the Angara.

•
02:03:05:18
02:03:08:10
Je n'ai jamais essayé.

•
02:03:05:18
02:03:08:10
I never tried.

	• 02:03:09:08 02:03:10:20
Но при чтении	Mas quando os lia,
	• 02:03:10:22 02:03:14:12
звучание названий рек всегда успокаивало меня.	o som dos seus nomes era sempre reconfortante.
	• 02:03:14:14 02:03:16:10
Словно их журчание.	Como os seus próprios murmúrios.
	• 02:03:17:02 02:03:19:04
Или тишина тайги.	Como a taiga que se balança.
	• 02:03:19:20 02:03:22:20
Шелест ветвей на верхушках кедра,	O movimento dos ramos superiores dos cedros,
	• 02:03:23:02 02:03:24:04
сосны,	pinheiros,

•
02:03:09:08
02:03:10:20
Mais lorsque je les lisais,

•
02:03:09:08
02:03:10:20
But when reading them,

•
02:03:10:22
02:03:14:12
les sonorités de ces noms
étaient toujours apaisantes.

•
02:03:10:22
02:03:12:08
the sound of their names
was always soothing.

•
02:03:14:14
02:03:16:10
Comme leurs propes murmures.

•
02:03:12:14
02:03:16:10
Like their own murmur.

•
02:03:17:02
02:03:19:04
Comme la taïga se balançant.

•
02:03:17:04
02:03:18:24
Like the taiga swooning.

•
02:03:19:20
02:03:22:20
Le mouvement
des branches supérieures du cèdre,

•
02:03:19:20
02:03:22:20
The movement of the top branches
of cedar,

•
02:03:23:02
02:03:24:04
du pin,

•
02:03:23:02
02:03:24:04
pine,

•
02:03:24:06
02:03:25:12

лиственницы,	larícios,

•
02:03:26:00
02:03:26:20

берёзы	bétulas,

•
02:03:27:00
02:03:28:04

и ели.	e abetos.

•
02:03:31:08
02:03:32:04

Каменушка,	Kamenuchka,

•
02:03:32:06
02:03:34:10

Сеннушка,	Sennuchka,

•
02:03:34:14
02:03:35:20

Банная,	Bánnaia,

•	•
02:03:24:06	02:03:24:06
02:03:25:12	02:03:25:12
du mélèze,	larch,
•	•
02:03:26:00	02:03:26:00
02:03:26:20	02:03:26:20
du bouleau,	birch,
•	•
02:03:27:00	02:03:27:00
02:03:28:04	02:03:28:04
et de l'épicéa.	and spruce.
•	•
02:03:31:08	02:03:31:08
02:03:32:04	02:03:32:04
Kamenoushka,	Kamenushka,
•	•
02:03:32:06	02:03:32:06
02:03:34:10	02:03:34:10
Sennoushka,	Sennushka,
•	•
02:03:34:14	02:03:34:14
02:03:35:20	02:03:35:20
Bannaïa,	Bannaya,

•

02:03:36:08
02:03:37:22

Крестовка, Krestovka,

•

02:03:38:00
02:03:40:02

Малая Черемшанка, Málaia Tcheremchanka,

•

02:03:40:23
02:03:43:00

Черемшанка, Tcheremchanka,

•

02:03:43:22
02:03:45:10

Смородовка, Smoródovka,

•

02:03:46:12
02:03:48:12

Средняя, Srédniaia,

•

02:03:49:02
02:03:50:20

Солонцова, Solontsova,

•

02:03:36:08
02:03:37:22
Krestovka,

•

02:03:38:00
02:03:40:02
Malaïa Cheremshanka,

•

02:03:40:23
02:03:43:00
Cheremshanka,

•

02:03:43:22
02:03:45:10
Smarodovka,

•

02:03:46:12
02:03:48:12
Srednyaïa,

•

02:03:49:02
02:03:50:20
Salantsova,

•

02:03:36:08
02:03:37:22
Krestovka,

•

02:03:38:00
02:03:40:02
Malaya Cheremshanka,

•

02:03:40:23
02:03:43:00
Cheremshanka,

•

02:03:43:22
02:03:45:10
Smorodovka,

•

02:03:46:12
02:03:48:12
Srednyaya,

•

02:03:49:02
02:03:50:20
Solontsova,

•

Чёрная, 02:03:52:04
02:03:53:12
Tchiórnaia,

•

Большие Коты, 02:03:54:18
02:03:57:02
Bolchie Koti,

•

Малые Коты, 02:03:58:18
02:04:00:08
Málie Koti,

•

Большая Сенная, 02:04:01:20
02:04:03:20
Bolchaia Sennaia,

•

Нижняя, 02:04:05:10
02:04:06:16
Níjniaia,

•

Большая Кадильная, 02:04:08:04
02:04:10:14
Bolchaia Kadílnaia,

•

02:03:52:04
02:03:53:12
Tchiornaïa,

•

02:03:54:18
02:03:57:02
Balshiye Katy,

•

02:03:58:18
02:04:00:08
Maliye Katy,

•

02:04:01:20
02:04:03:20
Balshaïa Sennaïa,

•

02:04:05:10
02:04:06:16
Nijnyaïa,

•

02:04:08:04
02:04:10:14
Balshaïa Kadilnaïa,

•

02:03:52:04
02:03:53:12
Chernaya,

•

02:03:54:18
02:03:57:02
Bolshiye Koty,

•

02:03:58:18
02:04:00:08
Maliye Koty,

•

02:04:01:20
02:04:03:20
Bolshaya Sennaya,

•

02:04:05:10
02:04:06:16
Nizhnyaya,

•

02:04:08:04
02:04:10:14
Bolshaya Kadilnaya,

•

02:04:11:22
02:04:13:22

Малая Кадильная, Málaia Kadílnaia,

•

02:04:15:14
02:04:17:14

Голоустная, Goloústnaia,

•

02:04:18:20
02:04:20:18

Правый Роговик, Právi Rogovik,

•

02:04:21:24
02:04:23:14

Еловка, Ielovka,

•

02:04:24:22
02:04:26:16

Шумиха, Chumikha,

•

02:04:28:08
02:04:29:20

Харгин, Kharguin,

•

02:04:11:22
02:04:13:22
Malaïa Kadilnaïa,

•

02:04:15:14
02:04:17:14
Galaoustnaïa,

•

02:04:18:20
02:04:20:18
Pravy Ragavic,

•

02:04:21:24
02:04:23:14
Ielovka,

•

02:04:24:22
02:04:26:16
Shoumikha,

•

02:04:28:08
02:04:29:20
Khargine,

•

02:04:11:22
02:04:13:22
Malaya Kadilnaya,

•

02:04:15:14
02:04:17:14
Goloustnaya,

•

02:04:18:20
02:04:20:18
Pravy Rogovic,

•

02:04:21:24
02:04:23:14
Yelovka,

•

02:04:24:22
02:04:26:16
Shumikha,

•

02:04:28:08
02:04:29:20
Khargin,

•

02:04:31:14
02:04:32:24

Лохматая, Lokhmátaia,

•

02:04:34:10
02:04:36:06

Ханхильтуй, Khankhiltui,

•

02:04:37:14
02:04:39:04

Сыксыхай, Siksikhai,

•

02:04:40:20
02:04:42:06

Куркера, Kurkera,

•

02:04:44:00
02:04:45:14

Курта, Kurta,

•

02:04:47:02
02:04:48:18

Бугульдейка, Buguldeika,

•

02:04:31:14
02:04:32:24
Lakhmataïa,

•

02:04:34:10
02:04:36:06
Khankhiltouï,

•

02:04:37:14
02:04:39:04
Syksyhaï,

•

02:04:40:20
02:04:42:06
Kourkera,

•

02:04:44:00
02:04:45:14
Kourta,

•

02:04:47:02
02:04:48:18
Bougouldeïka,

•

02:04:31:14
02:04:32:24
Lokhmataya,

•

02:04:34:10
02:04:36:06
Khankhiltui,

•

02:04:37:14
02:04:39:04
Syksyhai,

•

02:04:40:20
02:04:42:06
Kurkera,

•

02:04:44:00
02:04:45:14
Kurta,

•

02:04:47:02
02:04:48:18
Buguldeika,

•

02:04:50:08
02:04:53:16

Малая Бугульдейка или Таловка, Málaia Buguldeika ou Tálovka,

•

02:04:54:24
02:04:59:10

Зун-Кужирту или Зюн-Хожертуй, Zun-Kujirtu ou Ziun-Khojertui,

•

02:05:00:04
02:05:01:12

Марта, Marta,

•

02:05:02:16
02:05:04:22

Улан-Ганта, Ulan-Ganta,

•

02:05:06:10
02:05:08:10

Широкая, Chirókaia,

•

02:05:09:00
02:05:11:02

Крестовая, Krestóvaia,

•

02:04:50:08
02:04:53:16
Malaïa Bougouldeïka ou Talovka,

•

02:04:54:24
02:04:59:10
Zoun-Koujirtou ou
Zyoun-Khojertouï,

•

02:05:00:04
02:05:01:12
Marta,

•

02:05:02:16
02:05:04:22
Oulan-Ganta,

•

02:05:06:10
02:05:08:10
Shirokaïa,

•

02:05:09:00
02:05:11:02
Kristovaïa,

•

02:04:50:08
02:04:53:16
Malaya Buguldeika or Talovka,

•

02:04:54:24
02:04:59:10
Zun-Kuzhirtu or Zyun-Khozhertui,

•

02:05:00:04
02:05:01:12
Marta,

•

02:05:02:16
02:05:04:22
Ulan-Ganta,

•

02:05:06:10
02:05:08:10
Shirokaya,

•

02:05:09:00
02:05:11:02
Krestovka,

•

02:05:12:06
02:05:13:12

Бирхин, Birkhin,

•

02:05:15:14
02:05:16:20

Бегул, Begul,

•

02:05:18:08
02:05:19:12

Анга, Anga,

•

02:05:21:08
02:05:22:12

Халури, Khalúri,

•

02:05:24:04
02:05:25:18

Рассыпная, Rassipnaia,

•

02:05:27:14
02:05:28:20

Кучелга, Kutchelga,

•

02:05:12:06
02:05:13:12
Birkhine,

•

02:05:15:14
02:05:16:20
Bigoul,

•

02:05:18:08
02:05:19:12
Anga,

•

02:05:21:08
02:05:22:12
Khalouri,

•

02:05:24:04
02:05:25:18
Rassypnaïa,

•

02:05:27:14
02:05:28:20
Koutchelna,

•

02:05:12:06
02:05:13:12
Birkhin,

•

02:05:15:14
02:05:16:20
Begul,

•

02:05:18:08
02:05:19:12
Anga,

•

02:05:21:08
02:05:22:12
Khaluri,

•

02:05:24:04
02:05:25:18
Rassypnaya,

•

02:05:27:14
02:05:28:20
Kuchelga,

	•
	02:05:30:14
	02:05:31:22
Хорга,	Khorga,
	•
	02:05:33:04
	02:05:34:12
Сарма,	Sarma,
	•
	02:05:36:14
	02:05:37:24
Курма,	Kurma,
	•
	02:05:39:22
	02:05:44:00
Харанса или Харанца	Kharansa ou Kharantsa
	•
	02:05:45:02
	02:05:47:04
или Харанцинский,	ou Kharantsínski,
	•
	02:05:48:22
	02:05:52:18
Улан-Хын или Улан-Хан,	Ulan-Khin ou Ulan-Khan,

•
02:05:30:14
02:05:31:22
Khorgara,

•
02:05:30:14
02:05:31:22
Khorga,

•
02:05:33:04
02:05:34:12
Sarma,

•
02:05:33:04
02:05:34:12
Sarma,

•
02:05:36:14
02:05:37:24
Kourma,

•
02:05:36:14
02:05:37:24
Kurma,

•
02:05:39:22
02:05:44:00
Kharansa ou Kharantsa

•
02:05:39:22
02:05:44:00
Kharansa or Kharantsa

•
02:05:45:02
02:05:47:04
ou bien Kharantsinsky,

•
02:05:45:02
02:05:47:04
or Kharantsinsky,

•
02:05:48:22
02:05:52:18
Oulane-Khyne ou Oulane-Khane,

•
02:05:48:22
02:05:52:18
Ulan-Khyn or Ulan-Khan,

•

02:05:53:24
02:05:55:10

Отты, Otti,

•

02:05:56:10
02:05:57:22

Кормилица, Kormílitsa,

•

02:05:59:00
02:06:00:12

Зундук, Zunduk,

•

02:06:01:18
02:06:03:14

Кочерикова, Kotcherikova,

•

02:06:04:20
02:06:05:24

Хейрем, Kheirem,

•

02:06:07:10
02:06:09:10

Глубокая Падь, Glubókaia Pad,

•

02:05:53:24
02:05:55:10
Otty,

•

02:05:56:10
02:05:57:22
Karmilitsa,

•

02:05:59:00
02:06:00:12
Zoundouk,

•

02:06:01:18
02:06:03:14
Katcherikova,

•

02:06:04:20
02:06:05:24
Kheriem,

•

02:06:07:10
02:06:09:10
Gloubokaïa Pad,

•

02:05:53:24
02:05:55:10
Otty,

•

02:05:56:10
02:05:57:22
Kormilitsa,

•

02:05:59:00
02:06:00:12
Zundook,

•

02:06:01:18
02:06:03:14
Kocherikova,

•

02:06:04:20
02:06:05:24
Kheirem,

•

02:06:07:20
02:06:09:10
Glubokya Pad,

•

02:06:10:22
02:06:12:20

Солнце-Падь,	Solntse-Pad,

•

02:06:14:08
02:06:17:08

Рытая или Рита	Rítaia ou Rita

•

02:06:17:14
02:06:19:02

или Риты,	ou Ríti,

•

02:06:20:14
02:06:21:22

Анютка,	Aniutka,

•

02:06:23:02
02:06:24:12

Шартлан,	Chartlan,

•

02:06:26:00
02:06:27:18

Зеленовский,	Zelenóvski,

•	•
02:06:10:22	02:06:10:22
02:06:12:20	02:06:12:20
Solntse-Pad,	Solntse-Pad,
•	•
02:06:14:08	02:06:14:08
02:06:17:08	02:06:17:08
Ritaïa ou Rita	Rytya or Rita
•	•
02:06:17:14	02:06:17:14
02:06:19:02	02:06:19:02
ou bien Rite,	or Ryty,
•	•
02:06:20:14	02:06:20:14
02:06:21:22	02:06:21:22
Anyoutka,	Anyutka,
•	•
02:06:23:02	02:06:23:02
02:06:24:12	02:06:24:12
Shartlane,	Shartlan,
•	•
02:06:26:00	02:06:26:00
02:06:27:18	02:06:27:18
Zelenovsky,	Zelenovsky,

•

02:06:28:22
02:06:30:10

Элигей, Eliguei,

•

02:06:31:20
02:06:33:06

Ледяная, Ledianaia,

•

02:06:34:18
02:06:36:04

Елохин, Ielókhin,

•

02:06:37:10
02:06:38:24

Черемшанка, Tcheremchanka,

•

02:06:40:06
02:06:41:16

Светлый, Svétli,

•

02:06:43:02
02:06:44:12

Хибелен, Khibelen,

•

02:06:28:22
02:06:30:10
Eliguei,

•

02:06:28:22
02:06:30:10
Eligei,

•

02:06:31:20
02:06:33:06
Ledyanaïa,

•

02:06:31:20
02:06:33:06
Ledyanaya,

•

02:06:34:18
02:06:36:04
Yelokhine,

•

02:06:34:18
02:06:36:04
Yelokhin,

•

02:06:37:10
02:06:38:24
Cheremshanka,

•

02:06:37:10
02:06:38:24
Cheremshanka,

•

02:06:40:06
02:06:41:16
Svetly,

•

02:06:40:06
02:06:41:16
Svetly,

•

02:06:43:02
02:06:44:12
Khibelene,

•

02:06:43:02
02:06:44:12
Khibelen,

•

02:06:46:12
02:06:47:24

Малая Коса, Málaia Kossá,

•

02:06:49:00
02:06:51:02

Большая Коса, Bolchaia Kossá,

•

02:06:52:16
02:06:54:06

Мужинай, Mujinai,

•

02:06:55:14
02:06:57:02

Молокон, Molokon,

•

02:06:58:04
02:07:00:16

Татарниково Русло, Tatárnikovo Russlo,

•

02:07:01:22
02:07:03:24

Куркула, Kurkula,

•

02:06:46:12
02:06:47:24
Malaïa Kassa,

•

02:06:46:12
02:06:47:24
Malaya Kosa,

•

02:06:49:00
02:06:51:02
Balshaïa Kassa,

•

02:06:49:00
02:06:51:02
Bolshaya Rosa,

•

02:06:52:16
02:06:54:06
Moujinaï,

•

02:06:52:16
02:06:54:06
Muzhinai,

•

02:06:55:14
02:06:57:02
Malakone,

•

02:06:55:14
02:06:57:02
Molokon,

•

02:06:58:04
02:07:00:16
Tatarnikavo Roussla,

•

02:06:58:14
02:07:00:16
Tatarnikovo Ruslo,

•

02:07:01:22
02:07:03:24
Kourkoula,

•

02:07:01:22
02:07:03:24
Kurkula,

•

02:07:04:10
02:07:06:00

Горячая, Goriátchaia,

•

02:07:07:00
02:07:08:10

Гуилга, Guilga,

•

02:07:09:16
02:07:11:00

Горемыка, Goremika,

•

02:07:12:12
02:07:13:24

Талая, Tálaia,

•

02:07:14:20
02:07:16:18

Рель, Rel,

•

02:07:17:10
02:07:19:02

Слюдянка, Sliudianka,

•

02:07:04:10
02:07:06:00
Garyatchaïa,

•

02:07:07:00
02:07:08:10
Gouilga,

•

02:07:09:16
02:07:11:00
Goremyka,

•

02:07:12:12
02:07:13:24
Talaïa,

•

02:07:14:20
02:07:16:18
Rel,

•

02:07:17:10
02:07:19:02
Sliudianka,

•

02:07:04:10
02:07:06:00
Goryachaya,

•

02:07:07:00
02:07:08:10
Guilga,

•

02:07:09:16
02:07:11:00
Goremyka,

•

02:07:12:12
02:07:13:24
Talaya,

•

02:07:14:20
02:07:16:18
Rel,

•

02:07:17:10
02:07:19:02
Slyudyanka,

•

02:07:20:04
02:07:21:10

Сеногда,

Senogda,

•

02:07:22:10
02:07:23:14

Тыя,

Tíia,

•

02:07:24:21
02:07:25:22

Курла,

Kurla,

•

02:07:27:24
02:07:29:14

Туркин,

Turkin,

•

02:07:30:11
02:07:31:14

Тошка,

Tochka,

•

02:07:32:12
02:07:33:20

Кичера,

Kitchera,

•

02:07:20:04
02:07:21:10
Senagda,

•

02:07:22:10
02:07:23:14
Tiya,

•

02:07:24:21
02:07:25:22
Kourla,

•

02:07:27:24
02:07:29:14
Tourkine,

•

02:07:30:11
02:07:31:14
Toshka,

•

02:07:32:12
02:07:33:20
Kitchera,

•

02:07:20:04
02:07:21:10
Senogda,

•

02:07:22:10
02:07:23:14
Tyia,

•

02:07:24:21
02:07:25:22
Kurla,

•

02:07:27:24
02:07:29:14
Turkin,

•

02:07:30:11
02:07:31:14
Toshka,

•

02:07:32:12
02:07:33:20
Kichera,

•

02:07:34:22
02:07:36:18

Верхняя Ангара,	Vérkhniaia Angara,

•

02:07:38:00
02:07:39:20

Акуликан,	Akulikan,

•

02:07:40:20
02:07:42:04

Токшаки,	Tokchaki,

•

02:07:43:06
02:07:44:12

Ака,	Aka,

•

02:07:45:14
02:07:47:02

Биракан,	Birakan,

•

02:07:48:20
02:07:52:24

Эрекшакан или Рекшакан,	Erekchakan ou Rekchakan,

•

02:07:34:22
02:07:36:18
Vernyaïa Angara,

•

02:07:34:22
02:07:36:18
Verhnyaya Angara,

•

02:07:38:00
02:07:39:20
Akoulikane,

•

02:07:38:00
02:07:39:20
Akulikan,

•

02:07:40:20
02:07:42:04
Takshaki,

•

02:07:40:20
02:07:42:04
Tokshaki,

•

02:07:43:06
02:07:44:12
Aka,

•

02:07:43:06
02:07:44:12
Aka,

•

02:07:45:14
02:07:47:02
Birakane,

•

02:07:45:14
02:07:47:02
Birakan,

•

02:07:48:20
02:07:52:24
Erekshakane ou Rekshakane,

•

02:07:48:20
02:07:52:24
Erekshakan or Rekshakan,

•

02:07:54:20
02:07:56:20
Биракачан, Birakatchan,

•

02:07:58:02
02:07:59:12
Фролиха, Frolikha,

•

02:08:00:24
02:08:02:12
Аяя, Aiaia,

•

02:08:03:24
02:08:05:14
Тукалакан, Tukalakan,

•

02:08:07:08
02:08:09:06
Тукаларагды, Tukalaragdi,

•

02:08:10:24
02:08:14:02
Бирая или Берая, Biraia ou Beraia,

•

02:07:54:20
02:07:56:20
Birakatchane,

•

02:07:54:20
02:07:56:20
Birakachan,

•

02:07:58:02
02:07:59:12
Frolikha,

•

02:07:58:02
02:07:59:12
Frolikha,

•

02:08:00:24
02:08:02:12
Ayaïa,

•

02:08:00:24
02:08:02:12
Ayaya,

•

02:08:03:24
02:08:05:14
Toukalakane,

•

02:08:03:24
02:08:05:14
Tukalakan,

•

02:08:07:08
02:08:09:06
Toukalaragdy,

•

02:08:07:08
02:08:09:06
Tukalaragdy,

•

02:08:10:24
02:08:14:02
Biraïa ou Beraïa,

•

02:08:10:24
02:08:14:02
Biraya or Beraya,

•

02:08:15:24
02:08:17:08

Горячий,	Goriátchi,

•

02:08:18:22
02:08:20:10

Самдаки,	Samdaki,

•

02:08:21:24
02:08:23:14

Елшинский,	Ielchínski,

•

02:08:24:20
02:08:27:18

Сиригли или Ширильды,	Sirigli ou Chirildi,

•

02:08:29:06
02:08:32:16

Сельтикан или Селикан,	Seltikan ou Selikan,

•

02:08:33:16
02:08:36:06

Северный Амнундакан,	Séverni Amnundakan,

•

02:08:15:24
02:08:17:08
Garyatchi,

•

02:08:18:22
02:08:20:10
Samdaki,

•

02:08:21:24
02:08:23:14
Yelshinski,

•

02:08:24:20
02:08:27:18
Sirigly ou Shirildy,

•

02:08:29:06
02:08:32:16
Seltikane ou Selikane,

•

02:08:33:16
02:08:36:06
Severny Amnoundakane,

•

02:08:15:24
02:08:17:08
Goryachi,

•

02:08:18:22
02:08:20:10
Samdaki,

•

02:08:21:24
02:08:23:14
Yelshinski,

•

02:08:24:20
02:08:27:18
Sirigly or Shirildy,

•

02:08:29:06
02:08:32:16
Seltikan or Selikan,

•

02:08:33:16
02:08:36:06
Severny Amnundakan,

	• 02:08:37:07 02:08:40:02
Томпуда или Смолиха,	Tompuda ou Smolikha,
	• 02:08:41:16 02:08:43:02
Чувэр,	Tchuver,
	• 02:08:43:20 02:08:46:22
Шегнанда или Лабзиха,	Chegnanda ou Labzikha,
	• 02:08:48:04 02:08:49:24
Иринда,	Irinda,
	• 02:08:51:04 02:08:52:22
Ириндакан,	Irindakan,
	• 02:08:54:08 02:08:56:00
Урбикан,	Urbikane,

•

02:08:37:07
02:08:40:02
Tampouda ou Smalikha,

•

02:08:37:07
02:08:40:02
Tompuda or Smilokha,

•

02:08:41:16
02:08:43:02
Shouver,

•

02:08:41:16
02:08:43:02
Chuver,

•

02:08:43:20
02:08:46:22
Shignanda ou Labzikha,

•

02:08:43:20
02:08:46:22
Shegnanda or Labzikha,

•

02:08:48:04
02:08:49:24
Irinda,

•

02:08:48:04
02:08:49:24
Irinda,

•

02:08:51:04
02:08:52:22
Irindakane,

•

02:08:51:04
02:08:52:22
Irindakan,

•

02:08:54:08
02:08:56:00
Ourbikane,

•

02:08:54:08
02:08:56:00
Urbikan,

	•
	02:08:56:20
	02:08:58:16
Ботками,	Botkami,
	•
	02:09:00:00
	02:09:02:10
Северный Биракан,	Séverni Birakan,
	•
	02:09:03:16
	02:09:05:10
Якшакан,	Iakchakan,
	•
	02:09:06:00
	02:09:07:20
Кабанья,	Kabánia,
	•
	02:09:08:24
	02:09:10:16
Заезовочный,	Zaiezóvotchni,
	•
	02:09:12:00
	02:09:14:14
Езовка или Хаюла,	Iezovka ou Khaiula,

•

02:08:56:20
02:08:58:16
Batkami,

•

02:08:57:08
02:08:58:16
Botkami,

•

02:09:00:00
02:09:02:10
Severny Birakane,

•

02:09:00:10
02:09:02:10
Severny Birakan,

•

02:09:03:16
02:09:05:10
Yakshakane,

•

02:09:03:16
02:09:05:10
Yakshakan,

•

02:09:06:00
02:09:07:20
Kabaniya,

•

02:09:06:10
02:09:07:20
Kabaniya,

•

02:09:08:24
02:09:10:16
Zayezovatchny,

•

02:09:08:24
02:09:10:16
Zayezovochny,

•

02:09:12:00
02:09:14:14
Yezovka ou Khayoula,

•

02:09:12:00
02:09:14:14
Yezovka or Khayula,

•

02:09:16:00
02:09:18:06

Куркавка,

Kurkavka,

•

02:09:19:16
02:09:22:02

Большая или Ирба,

Bolchaia ou Irba,

•

02:09:24:00
02:09:25:16

Дугульдзеры,

Duguldzeri,

•

02:09:26:20
02:09:29:14

Давша или Давше,

Davcha ou Davche,

•

02:09:30:24
02:09:33:00

Южный Биракан,

Iújni Birakan,

•

02:09:34:07
02:09:35:22

Таркулик,

Tarkulik,

•

02:09:16:00
02:09:18:06
Kourkavka,

•

02:09:19:16
02:09:22:02
Balshaïa ou Irba,

•

02:09:24:00
02:09:25:16
Dougouldzery,

•

02:09:26:20
02:09:29:14
Davsha ou Davshe,

•

02:09:30:24
02:09:33:00
Youjny Birakane,

•

02:09:34:07
02:09:35:22
Tarkoulik,

•

02:09:16:22
02:09:18:06
Kurkavka,

•

02:09:19:16
02:09:22:02
Bolshaya or Irba,

•

02:09:24:00
02:09:25:16
Duguldzery,

•

02:09:26:20
02:09:29:14
Davsha or Davshe,

•

02:09:30:24
02:09:33:00
Yuzhny Birakan,

•

02:09:34:07
02:09:35:22
Tarkulik,

•

02:09:36:20
02:09:38:06
Кабалик, Kabalik,

•

02:09:39:22
02:09:41:12
Одорчонка, Odortchionka,

•

02:09:43:02
02:09:44:20
Сосновка, Sosnovka,

•

02:09:45:18
02:09:47:10
Межевой, Mejevói,

•

02:09:48:10
02:09:49:22
Кудалды, Kudaldi,

•

02:09:51:14
02:09:53:08
Налимиха, Nalímikha,

•

02:09:36:20
02:09:38:06
Kabalik,

•

02:09:36:20
02:09:38:06
Kabalik,

•

02:09:39:22
02:09:41:12
Adartchionka,

•

02:09:39:22
02:09:41:12
Odorchonka,

•

02:09:43:02
02:09:44:20
Sasnovka,

•

02:09:43:02
02:09:44:20
Sosnovka,

•

02:09:45:18
02:09:47:10
Mezhevoï,

•

02:09:45:18
02:09:47:10
Mezhevoi,

•

02:09:48:10
02:09:49:22
Koudaldy,

•

02:09:48:10
02:09:49:22
Kudaldy,

•

02:09:51:14
02:09:53:08
Nalimikha,

•

02:09:51:14
02:09:53:08
Nalimikha,

•

	02:09:54:08 02:09:55:24
Шумилиха,	Chumílikha,

•

	02:09:57:10 02:09:58:22
Воронинский,	Voróninski,

•

	02:09:59:16 02:10:01:14
Громотуха,	Gromotukha,

•

	02:10:02:14 02:10:04:04
Скалистый,	Skalísti,

•

	02:10:05:18 02:10:07:08
Власовский,	Vlássovski,

•

	02:10:08:02 02:10:10:02
Межевой,	Mejevói,

•

02:09:54:08
02:09:55:24
Shoumilikha,

•

02:09:54:08
02:09:55:24
Shumilikha,

•

02:09:57:10
02:09:58:22
Varoninski,

•

02:09:57:10
02:09:58:22
Voroninski,

•

02:09:59:16
02:10:01:14
Garmatoukha,

•

02:09:59:24
02:10:01:14
Gromotukha,

•

02:10:02:14
02:10:04:04
Skalisty,

•

02:10:02:14
02:10:04:04
Skalisty,

•

02:10:05:18
02:10:07:08
Vlasovski,

•

02:10:05:18
02:10:07:08
Vlasovski,

•

02:10:08:02
02:10:10:02
Mejevoï,

•

02:10:08:12
02:10:10:02
Mezhevoi,

•

02:10:11:04
02:10:13:10

Большая Черемшана, Bolchaia Tcheremchana,

•

02:10:14:02
02:10:15:16

Золотой, Zolotói,

•

02:10:16:16
02:10:18:24

Малая Черемшана, Málaia Tcheremchana,

•

02:10:19:16
02:10:21:12

Кедровая, Kedróvaia,

•

02:10:21:22
02:10:23:20

Большая Сухая, Bolchaia Sukhaia,

•

02:10:24:20
02:10:26:12

Малая Сухая, Málaia Sukhaia,

•

02:10:11:04
02:10:13:10
Balshaya Cheremshana,

•

02:10:14:02
02:10:15:16
Zalatoï,

•

02:10:16:16
02:10:18:24
Malaïa Cheremshana,

•

02:10:19:16
02:10:21:12
Kedrovaïa,

•

02:10:21:22
02:10:23:20
Balshaïa Soukhaïa,

•

02:10:24:20
02:10:26:12
Malaïa Soukhaïa,

•

02:10:11:04
02:10:13:10
Bolshaya Cheremshana,

•

02:10:14:02
02:10:15:16
Zolotoi,

•

02:10:17:04
02:10:18:24
Malaya Cheremshana,

•

02:10:19:16
02:10:21:12
Kedrovaya,

•

02:10:21:22
02:10:23:20
Bolshaya Sukhaya,

•

02:10:24:20
02:10:26:12
Malaya Sukhaya,

•

02:10:27:14
02:10:30:00
Большой Чивыркуй, Bolchói Tchivirkui,

•

02:10:30:12
02:10:32:02
Безымянная, Bezimiánnaia,

•

02:10:33:12
02:10:35:12
Малый Чивыркуй, Máli Tchivirkui,

•

02:10:37:04
02:10:38:22
Крохалиная, Krokhalínaia,

•

02:10:40:08
02:10:42:00
Крестовская, Krestóvskaia,

•

02:10:43:18
02:10:45:06
Маршалиха, Marchálikha,

•

02:10:27:14
02:10:30:00
Balshoï Tchivyrkouï,

•

02:10:30:12
02:10:32:02
Bezymyannaïa,

•

02:10:33:12
02:10:35:12
Malyi Tchivyrkouï,

•

02:10:37:04
02:10:38:22
Krokhalinaïa,

•

02:10:40:08
02:10:42:00
Krestovskaïa,

•

02:10:43:18
02:10:45:06
Marshalikha,

•

02:10:27:14
02:10:30:00
Bolshoi Chivyrkui,

•

02:10:30:12
02:10:32:02
Bezymyannaya,

•

02:10:33:12
02:10:35:12
Malyi Chivyrkui,

•

02:10:37:04
02:10:38:22
Krokhalinaya,

•

02:10:40:08
02:10:42:00
Krestovskaya,

•

02:10:43:18
02:10:45:06
Marshalikha,

•

02:10:46:20
02:10:48:20

Онгокон, Ongokon,

•

02:10:50:10
02:10:51:22

Молодость, Mólodost,

•

02:10:53:08
02:10:54:16

Маркова, Márkova,

•

02:10:56:04
02:10:57:14

Макарова, Makárova,

•

02:10:59:08
02:11:01:08

Буртуй, Burtui,

•

02:11:02:20
02:11:04:08

Баргузин, Barguzin,

•

02:10:46:20
02:10:48:20
Ongokone,

•

02:10:46:20
02:10:48:20
Ongokon,

•

02:10:50:10
02:10:51:22
Molodost,

•

02:10:50:10
02:10:51:22
Molodost,

•

02:10:53:08
02:10:54:16
Markova,

•

02:10:53:08
02:10:54:16
Markova,

•

02:10:56:04
02:10:57:14
Makarova,

•

02:10:56:04
02:10:57:14
Makarova,

•

02:10:59:08
02:11:01:08
Bourtouï,

•

02:10:59:08
02:11:01:08
Burtui,

•

02:11:02:20
02:11:04:08
Bargouzine,

•

02:11:02:20
02:11:04:08
Barguzin,

•

02:11:05:24
02:11:07:16

Духовая, Dukhovaia,

•

02:11:08:14
02:11:10:10

Максимиха, Maksímikha,

•

02:11:11:08
02:11:12:24

Громотуха, Gromotukha,

•

02:11:14:08
02:11:15:20

Киселева, Kisseliova,

•

02:11:17:04
02:11:18:08

Средний, Srédni,

•

02:11:19:18
02:11:21:10

Телегинский, Teleguínski,

•

02:11:05:24
02:11:07:16
Doukhavaïa,

•

02:11:05:24
02:11:07:16
Dukhovaya,

•

02:11:08:14
02:11:10:10
Maksimikha,

•

02:11:08:14
02:11:10:10
Maksimikha,

•

02:11:11:08
02:11:12:24
Gramatoukha,

•

02:11:11:08
02:11:12:24
Gromotukha,

•

02:11:14:08
02:11:15:20
Kiseliova,

•

02:11:14:08
02:11:15:20
Kiseleva,

•

02:11:17:04
02:11:18:08
Srednyi,

•

02:11:17:04
02:11:18:08
Srednyi,

•

02:11:19:18
02:11:21:10
Teleginski,

•

02:11:19:18
02:11:21:10
Teleginski,

•

02:11:22:12
02:11:24:04

Белокаменский,	Belokámenski,

•

02:11:25:18
02:11:27:16

Каткова,	Katkova,

•

02:11:28:23
02:11:30:15

Елисеевский,	Ielisséevski,

•

02:11:32:02
02:11:35:02

Безымянка или Безымянная,	Bezimianka ou Bezimiánnaia,

•

02:11:36:14
02:11:38:04

Налимовка,	Nalímovka,

•

02:11:39:12
02:11:41:06

Черемшанка,	Tcheremchanka,

•

02:11:22:12
02:11:24:04
Belakamenski,

•

02:11:22:12
02:11:24:04
Belokamenski,

•

02:11:25:18
02:11:27:16
Katkova,

•

02:11:25:18
02:11:27:16
Katkova,

•

02:11:28:23
02:11:30:15
Yeliseyevski,

•

02:11:28:23
02:11:30:15
Yeliseyevski,

•

02:11:32:02
02:11:35:02
Bezymyanka ou Bezymyannaïa,

•

02:11:32:02
02:11:35:02
Bezymyanka or Bezymyannaya,

•

02:11:36:14
02:11:38:04
Nalimovka,

•

02:11:36:14
02:11:38:04
Nalimovka,

•

02:11:39:12
02:11:41:06
Cheremshanka,

•

02:11:39:12
02:11:41:06
Cheremshanka,

•

02:11:42:10
02:11:44:04
Шивелевский, Chivelévski,

•

02:11:45:10
02:11:46:20
Турка, Turka,

•

02:11:48:00
02:11:49:10
Кика, Kika,

•

02:11:51:06
02:11:53:06
Рассыпная, Rassipnaia,

•

02:11:54:00
02:11:55:10
Долгий, Dólgi,

•

02:11:56:08
02:11:57:20
Песчанка, Pestchanka,

•

02:11:42:10
02:11:44:04
Shevelevski,

•

02:11:42:10
02:11:44:04
Shevelevski,

•

02:11:45:10
02:11:46:20
Tourka,

•

02:11:45:10
02:11:46:20
Turka,

•

02:11:48:00
02:11:49:10
Kicka,

•

02:11:48:00
02:11:49.10
Kicka,

•

02:11:51:06
02:11:53:06
Rassypnaïa,

•

02:11:51:06
02:11:53:06
Rassypnaya,

•

02:11:54:00
02:11:55:10
Dolgyi,

•

02:11:54:00
02:11:55:10
Dolgyi,

•

02:11:56:08
02:11:57:20
Pestchanka,

•

02:11:56:08
02:11:57:20
Peschanka,

•

02:11:59:02
02:12:00:20
Таланчанка, Talantchanka,

•

02:12:01:20
02:12:03:16
Черемшанка, Tcheremchanka,

•

02:12:04:16
02:12:06:16
Малая Сухая, Málaia Sukhaia,

•

02:12:08:00
02:12:09:24
Капустинская, Kapústinskaia,

•

02:12:11:02
02:12:13:22
Большая Зеленовская, Bolchaia Zelenóvskaia,

•

02:12:14:02
02:12:16:08
Малая Зеленовская, Málaia Zelenóvskaia,

•

02:11:59:02
02:12:00:20
Talantchanka,

•

02:12:01:20
02:12:03:16
Tcheremshanka,

•

02:12:04:16
02:12:06:16
Malaïa Soukhaïa,

•

02:12:08:00
02:12:09:24
Kapoustinskaïa,

•

02:12:11:02
02:12:13:22
Balshaïa Zelenovskaïa,

•

02:12:14:02
02:12:16:08
Malaïa Zelenovskaïa,

•

02:11:59:02
02:12:00:20
Talanchanka,

•

02:12:01:20
02:12:03:16
Cheremshanka,

•

02:12:04:16
02:12:06:16
Malaya Sukhaya,

•

02:12:08:00
02:12:09:24
Kapustinskaya,

•

02:12:11:02
02:12:13:22
Bolshaya Zelenovskaya,

•

02:12:14:02
02:12:16:08
Malaya Zelenovskaya,

•

02:12:17:18
02:12:19:08

Колодянка, Kolodianka,

•

02:12:20:12
02:12:22:08

Болдаковка, Boldakovka,

•

02:12:23:08
02:12:25:00

Стволовая, Stvolovaia,

•

02:12:25:24
02:12:27:24

Большая Сухая, Bolchaia Sukhaia,

•

02:12:29:04
02:12:30:10

Топка, Topka,

•

02:12:31:18
02:12:32:22

Загза, Zagza,

•

02:12:17:18
02:12:19:08
Kaladyanka,

•

02:12:17:18
02:12:19:08
Kolodyanka,

•

02:12:20:12
02:12:22:08
Baldakovka,

•

02:12:20:12
02:12:22:08
Boldakovka,

•

02:12:23:08
02:12:25:00
Stvolovaïa,

•

02:12:23:08
02:12:25:00
Stvolovaya,

•

02:12:25:24
02:12:27:24
Balshaïa Soukhaïa,

•

02:12:25:24
02:12:27:24
Bolshaya Sukhaya,

•

02:12:29:04
02:12:30:10
Topka,

•

02:12:29:04
02:12:30:10
Topka,

•

02:12:31:18
02:12:32:22
Zagza,

•

02:12:31:18
02:12:32:22
Zagza,

•

02:12:34:02
02:12:35:18
Энхелук, Enkheluk,

•

02:12:36:14
02:12:38:06
Большой Дулан, Bolchói Dulan,

•

02:12:39:00
02:12:40:06
Оймур, Oimur,

•

02:12:41:22
02:12:43:16
Сырая Молька, Siraia Molka,

•

02:12:45:02
02:12:46:16
Селенга, Selenga,

•

02:12:48:04
02:12:49:12
Шумиха, Chumikha,

•

02:12:34:02
02:12:35:18
Enkhelouk,

•

02:12:36:14
02:12:38:06
Balshoï Doulane,

•

02:12:39:00
02:12:40:06
Oïmour,

•

02:12:41:22
02:12:43:16
Syraïa Molka,

•

02:12:45:02
02:12:46:16
Selenga,

•

02:12:48:04
02:12:49:12
Shoumikha,

•

02:12:34:02
02:12:35:18
Enkheluk,

•

02:12:36:14
02:12:38:06
Bolshoi Dulan,

•

02:12:39:00
02:12:40:06
Oimur,

•

02:12:41:22
02:12:43:16
Syraya Molka,

•

02:12:45:02
02:12:46:16
Selenga,

•

02:12:48:04
02:12:49:12
Shumikha,

•

02:12:51:12
02:12:53:00

Исток,	Istok,

•

02:12:54:16
02:12:56:12

Большая Речка,	Bolchaia Retchka,

•

02:12:57:22
02:13:01:10

Толбозиха или Толбузиха	Tolbozikha ou Tolbuzikha

•

02:13:02:06
02:13:04:02

или Толбажиха,	ou Tolbajikha,

•

02:13:06:02
02:13:07:10

Абрамиха,	Abrámikha,

•

02:13:09:06
02:13:11:10

Большая Култушная,	Bolchaia Kultúchnaia,

- 02:12:51:12
02:12:53:00
Istok,

- 02:12:54:16
02:12:56:12
Balshaïa Rechka,

- 02:12:57:22
02:13:01:10
Talbozikha ou Talbouzikha

- 02:13:02:06
02:13:04:02
ou bien Talbajikha,

- 02:13:06:02
02:13:07:10
Abramikha,

- 02:13:09:06
02:13:11:10
Balshaïa Koultoushnaïa,

- 02:12:51:12
02:12:53:00
Istok,

- 02:12:54:16
02:12:56:12
Bolshaya Rechka,

- 02:12:57:22
02:13:01:10
Tolbozikha or Tolbuzikha

- 02:13:02:06
02:13:04:02
or Tolbazhikha,

- 02:13:06:02
02:13:07:10
Abramikha,

- 02:13:09:06
02:13:11:10
Bolshaya Kultushnaya,

•

02:13:12:20
02:13:14:06

Боярский, Boiárski,

•

02:13:15:22
02:13:17:06

Сухой Ручей, Sukhói Rutchei,

•

02:13:18:24
02:13:20:10

Мантуриха, Mantúrikha,

•

02:13:21:18
02:13:23:02

Гремучий, Gremútchi,

•

02:13:24:20
02:13:26:12

Малая Тельная, Málaia Télnaia,

•

02:13:28:02
02:13:29:24

Большая Тельная, Bolchaia Télnaia,

•

02:13:12:20
02:13:14:06
Bayarski,

•

02:13:12:20
02:13:14:06
Boyarski,

•

02:13:15:22
02:13:17:06
Soukhoï Routcheï,

•

02:13:15:22
02:13:17:06
Sukhoi Ruchei,

•

02:13:18:24
02:13:20:10
Mantourikha,

•

02:13:18:24
02:13:20:10
Manturikha,

•

02:13:21:18
02:13:23:02
Gremoutchi,

•

02:13:21:18
02:13:23:02
Gremuchi,

•

02:13:24:20
02:13:26:12
Malaïa Telnaïa,

•

02:13:24:20
02:13:26:12
Malaya Telnaya,

•

02:13:28:02
02:13:29:24
Balshaïa Telnaïa,

•

02:13:28:02
02:13:29:24
Bolshaya Telnaya,

•

02:13:31:20
02:13:33:10

Чукчанка, Tchuktchanka,

•

02:13:34:24
02:13:36:18

Мысовка, Missovka,

•

02:13:37:24
02:13:40:00

Малая Осиновка, Málaia Ossínovka,

•

02:13:41:08
02:13:43:16

Большая Осиновка, Bolchaia Ossínovka,

•

02:13:45:06
02:13:46:24

Калтусная, Kaltúsnaia,

•

02:13:48:12
02:13:49:24

Клюевка, Kliúevka,

•

02:13:31:20
02:13:33:10
Choukchanka,

•

02:13:34:24
02:13:36:18
Mysovka,

•

02:13:37:24
02:13:40:00
Malaïa Asinovka,

•

02:13:41:08
02:13:43:16
Balshaïa Asinovka,

•

02:13:45:06
02:13:46:24
Kaltousnaïa,

•

02:13:48:12
02:13:49:24
Kliouyevka,

•

02:13:31:20
02:13:33:10
Chukchanka,

•

02:13:34:24
02:13:36:18
Mysovka,

•

02:13:37:24
02:13:40:00
Malaya Osinovka,

•

02:13:41:08
02:13:43:16
Bolshaya Osinovka,

•

02:13:45:06
02:13:46:24
Kaltusnaya,

•

02:13:48:12
02:13:49:24
Klyuyevka,

•

02:13:51:08
02:13:53:06
Большая Ивановка, Bolchaia Ivánovka,

•

02:13:54:06
02:13:55:24
Малая Ивановка, Málaia Ivánovka,

•

02:13:57:02
02:13:58:24
Крестовка, Krestovka,

•

02:14:00:12
02:14:01:22
Ореховка, Orékhovka,

•

02:14:03:20
02:14:05:10
Быстрая, Bístraia,

•

02:14:07:04
02:14:08:18
Калтусная, Kaltúsnaia,

•

02:13:51:08
02:13:53:06
Balshaïa Ivanovka,

•

02:13:54:06
02:13:55:24
Malaïa Ivanovka,

•

02:13:57:02
02:13:58:24
Krestovka,

•

02:14:00:12
02:14:01:22
Arekhovka,

•

02:14:03:20
02:14:05:10
Bistraïa,

•

02:14:07:04
02:14:08:18
Kaltousnaïa,

•

02:13:51:08
02:13:53:06
Bolshaya Ivanovka,

•

02:13:54:06
02:13:55:24
Malaya Ivanovka,

•

02:13:57:02
02:13:58:24
Krestovka,

•

02:14:00:12
02:14:01:22
Orekhovka,

•

02:14:03:20
02:14:05:10
Bistraya,

•

02:14:07:04
02:14:08:18
Kaltusnaya,

	•
	02:14:10:12
	02:14:12:10
Болваниха,	Bolvánikha,
	•
	02:14:13:24
	02:14:15:14
Мишиха,	Michikha,
	•
	02:14:17:04
	02:14:19:06
Большая Язовка,	Bolchaia Iázovka,
	•
	02:14:20:14
	02:14:22:10
Малая Язовка,	Málaia Iázovka,
	•
	02:14:24:06
	02:14:26:04
Ушаковка,	Uchakovka,
	•
	02:14:27:18
	02:14:29:18
Осиновка,	Ossínovka,

•
02:14:10:12
02:14:12:10
Balvanikha,

•
02:14:10:12
02:14:12:10
Bolvanikha,

•
02:14:13:24
02:14:15:14
Mishikha,

•
02:14:13:24
02:14:15:14
Mishikha,

•
02:14:17:04
02:14:19:06
Balshaïa Yazovka,

•
02:14:17:04
02:14:19:06
Bolshaya Yazovka,

•
02:14:20:14
02:14:22:10
Malaïa Yazovka,

•
02:14:20:14
02:14:22:10
Malaya Yazovka,

•
02:14:24:06
02:14:26:04
Oushakovka,

•
02:14:24:06
02:14:26:04
Ushakovka,

•
02:14:27:18
02:14:29:18
Asinovka,

•
02:14:27:18
02:14:29:18
Osinovka,

•

02:14:30:20
02:14:32:12

Малиновка, Malínovka,

•

02:14:34:02
02:14:35:24

Половинка, Polovinka,

•

02:14:37:12
02:14:39:08

Куркавочная, Kurkávotchnaia,

•

02:14:40:22
02:14:42:12

Калтусная, Kaltúsnaia,

•

02:14:43:16
02:14:45:06

Переемная, Pereiémnaia,

•

02:14:46:22
02:14:48:12

Безголовка, Bezgolovka,

•

02:14:30:20
02:14:32:12
Malinovka,

•

02:14:30:20
02:14:32:12
Malinovka,

•

02:14:34:02
02:14:35:24
Palavinka,

•

02:14:34:02
02:14:35:24
Polovinka,

•

02:14:37:12
02:14:39:08
Kourkavotchnaïa,

•

02:14:37:12
02:14:39:08
Kurkavochnaya,

•

02:14:40:22
02:14:42:12
Kaltousnaïa,

•

02:14:40:22
02:14:42:12
Kaltusnaya,

•

02:14:43:16
02:14:45:06
Pereyemnaïa,

•

02:14:43:16
02:14:45:06
Pereyemnaya,

•

02:14:46:22
02:14:48:12
Bezgalovka,

•

02:14:46:22
02:14:48:12
Bezgolovka,

•

02:14:49:22
02:14:51:10

Осиновка,	Ossínovka,

•

02:14:53:02
02:14:54:20

Шестопалиха,	Chestopálikha,

•

02:14:56:20
02:14:58:08

Селенгушка,	Selenguchka,

•

02:14:59:22
02:15:01:10

Дулиха,	Dulikha,

•

02:15:03:10
02:15:05:02

Аносовка,	Anóssovka,

•

02:15:07:06
02:15:08:24

Куркавка,	Kurkavka,

•

02:14:49:22
02:14:51:10
Asinovka,

•

02:14:49:22
02:14:51:10
Osinovka,

•

02:14:53:02
02:14:54:20
Shestapalikha,

•

02:14:53:02
02:14:54:20
Shestopalikha,

•

02:14:56:20
02:14:58:08
Selengoushka,

•

02:14:56:20
02:14:58:08
Selengushka,

•

02:14:59:22
02:15:01:10
Doulikha,

•

02:14:59:22
02:15:01:10
Dulikha,

•

02:15:03:10
02:15:05:02
Anosovka,

•

02:15:03:10
02:15:05:02
Anosovka,

•

02:15:07:06
02:15:08:24
Kourkavka,

•

02:15:07:06
02:15:08:24
Kurkavka,

	•
	02:15:10:16
	02:15:12:02
Осиновка,	Ossínovka,
	•
	02:15:13:14
	02:15:14:24
Выдриная,	Vídrinaia,
	•
	02:15:16:18
	02:15:18:06
Малый Мамай,	Máli Mamai,
	•
	02:15:19:20
	02:15:21:06
Большой Мамай,	Bolchoi Mamai,
	•
	02:15:22:22
	02:15:24:14
Осиновка,	Ossínovka,
	•
	02:15:25:06
	02:15:26:22
Толбозиха,	Tolbozikha,

•

02:15:10:16
02:15:12:02
Asinovka,

•

02:15:10:16
02:15:12:02
Osinovka,

•

02:15:13:14
02:15:14:24
Vydrinaïa,

•

02:15:13:14
02:15:14:24
Vydrinaya,

•

02:15:16:18
02:15:18:06
Malyi Mamaï,

•

02:15:16:18
02:15:18:06
Malyi Mamai,

•

02:15:19:20
02:15:21:06
Balshoï Mamaï,

•

02:15:19:20
02:15:21:06
Bolshoi Mamai,

•

02:15:22:22
02:15:24:14
Asinovka,

•

02:15:22:22
02:15:24:14
Osinovka,

•

02:15:25:06
02:15:26:22
Tolbazikha,

•

02:15:25:06
02:15:26:22
Tolbozikha,

•

02:15:28:06
02:15:29:12

Снежная, Snéjnaia,

•

02:15:31:08
02:15:32:24

Малые Мангилы, Málie Manguíli,

•

02:15:34:12
02:15:36:12

Большие Мангилы, Bolchie Manguíli,

•

02:15:38:08
02:15:42:08

Паньковка или Паньковская, Pankovka ou Pankóvskaia,

•

02:15:43:18
02:15:45:08

Хара-Мурин, Khara-Murin,

•

02:15:46:22
02:15:48:04

Пьяный, Piáni,

•

02:15:28:06
02:15:29:12
Snejnaïa,

•

02:15:31:08
02:15:32:24
Maliye Mangily,

•

02:15:34:12
02:15:36:12
Balshiye Mangily,

•

02:15:38:08
02:15:42:08
Pankovka ou Pankovskaïa,

•

02:15:43:18
02:15:45:08
Khara-Mourine,

•

02:15:46:22
02:15:48:04
Pyanyi,

•

02:15:28:06
02:15:29:12
Snezhnaya,

•

02:15:31:08
02:15:32:24
Maliye Mangily,

•

02:15:34:12
02:15:36:12
Bolshiye Mangily,

•

02:15:38:08
02:15:42:08
Pankovka or Pankovskaya,

•

02:15:43:18
02:15:45:08
Khara-Murin,

•

02:15:46:22
02:15:48:04
Pyanyi,

•

02:15:49:22
02:15:51:12
Ширингаиха, Chiringaikha,

•

02:15:53:14
02:15:55:02
Семиречка, Semiretchka,

•

02:15:57:06
02:15:59:16
Банный, Bánni,

•

02:16:00:00
02:16:01:08
Ямный, Iámni,

•

02:16:03:16
02:16:05:12
Малая Осиновка, Málaia Ossínovka,

•

02:16:07:02
02:16:09:06
Большая Осиновка, Bolchaia Ossínovka,

•
02:15:49:22
02:15:51:12
Shiringaïkha,

•
02:15:49:22
02:15:51:12
Shiringaikha,

•
02:15:53:14
02:15:55:02
Semirechka,

•
02:15:53:14
02:15:55:02
Semirechka,

•
02:15:57:06
02:15:59:16
Bannyi,

•
02:15:57:06
02:15:59:16
Bannyi,

•
02:16:00:00
02:16:01:08
Yamnyi,

•
02:16:00:00
02:16:01:08
Yamnyi,

•
02:16:03:16
02:16:05:12
Malaïa Asinovka,

•
02:16:03:16
02:16:05:12
Malaya Osinovka,

•
02:16:07:02
02:16:09:06
Balshaïa Asinovka,

•
02:16:07:02
02:16:09:06
Bolshaya Osinovka,

•

02:16:10:14
02:16:11:22

Солзан,	Solzan,

•

02:16:14:06
02:16:15:20

Харлахта,	Kharlakhta,

•

02:16:17:16
02:16:18:24

Красный,	Krásni,

•

02:16:20:10
02:16:22:04

Межевой,	Mejevói,

•

02:16:23:16
02:16:25:06

Болотный,	Bolótni,

•

02:16:27:06
02:16:28:14

Бабха,	Babkha,

- 02:16:10:14
  02:16:11:22
  Solzane,

- 02:16:14:06
  02:16:15:20
  Kharlakhta,

- 02:16:17:16
  02:16:18:24
  Krasnyi,

- 02:16:20:10
  02:16:22:04
  Mejevoï,

- 02:16:23:16
  02:16:25:06
  Balotnyi,

- 02:16:27:06
  02:16:28:14
  Babkha,

- 02:16:10:14
  02:16:11:22
  Solzan,

- 02:16:14:06
  02:16:15:20
  Kharlakhta,

- 02:16:17:16
  02:16:18:24
  Krasnyi,

- 02:16:20:10
  02:16:22:04
  Mezhevoi,

- 02:16:23:16
  02:16:25:06
  Bolotnyi,

- 02:16:27:06
  02:16:28:14
  Babkha,

•

02:16:30:14
02:16:31:22

Утулик, Utulik,

•

02:16:33:16
02:16:35:06

Ермолаевский, Iermoláevski,

•

02:16:37:06
02:16:39:08

Большая Куркавочная, Bochaia Kurkávotchnaia,

•

02:16:41:00
02:16:42:12

Скачкова, Skatchkova,

•

02:16:44:04
02:16:45:14

Голанский, Golanski,

•

02:16:47:04
02:16:49:06

Безымянная, Bezimiánnaia,

•

02:16:30:14
02:16:31:22
Outoulik,

•

02:16:33:16
02:16:35:06
Yermolayevski,

•

02:16:37:06
02:16:39:08
Balshaïa Kourkavochnaïa,

•

02:16:41:00
02:16:42:12
Skachkova,

•

02:16:44:04
02:16:45:14
Galanski,

•

02:16:47:04
02:16:49:06
Besymyannaïa,

•

02:16:30:14
02:16:31:22
Utulik,

•

02:16:33:16
02:16:35:06
Yermolayevski,

•

02:16:37:06
02:16:39:08
Bolshaya Kurkavochnaya,

•

02:16:41:00
02:16:42:12
Skachkova,

•

02:16:44:04
02:16:45:14
Golanski,

•

02:16:47:04
02:16:49:06
Besymyannaya,

•

02:16:50:12
02:16:51:24

Буровщина,

Burówchina,

•

02:16:53:12
02:16:54:24

Сухой,

Sukhói,

•

02:16:56:10
02:16:57:18

Слюдянка,

Sliudianka,

•

02:16:59:08
02:17:00:22

Похабиха,

Pokhábikha,

•

02:17:02:02
02:17:03:16

Талая,

Tálaia,

•

02:17:04:24
02:17:06:08

Култучная,

Kultútchnaia,

•

02:16:50:12
02:16:51:24
Bourovshina,

•

02:16:53:12
02:16:54:24
Soukhoï,

•

02:16:56:10
02:16:57:18
Slyoudyanka,

•

02:16:59:08
02:17:00:22
Pakhabikha,

•

02:17:02:02
02:17:03:16
Talaïa,

•

02:17:04:24
02:17:06:08
Koultouchnaïa,

•

02:16:50:12
02:16:51:24
Burovshina,

•

02:16:53:12
02:16:54:24
Sukhoi,

•

02:16:56:10
02:16:57:18
Slyudyanka,

•

02:16:59:08
02:17:00:22
Pokhabikha,

•

02:17:02:02
02:17:03:16
Talaya,

•

02:17:04:24
02:17:06:08
Kultuchnaya,

•

02:17:07:16
02:17:09:02
Медлянка, Medlianka,

•

02:17:11:00
02:17:12:18
Ангасолка, Angassolka,

•

02:17:14:18
02:17:16:04
Хабартуй, Khabartui,

•

02:17:17:20
02:17:20:10
Большая Крутая Губа, Bolchaia Krutaia Gubá,

•

02:17:21:18
02:17:23:20
Малая Крутая Губа, Málaia Krutaia Gubá,

•

02:17:25:16
02:17:27:06
Шарыжалгай, Charijalgai,

•

02:17:07:16
02:17:09:02
Medlyanka,

•

02:17:11:00
02:17:12:18
Angasolka,

•

02:17:14:18
02:17:16:04
Khabartouï,

•

02:17:17:20
02:17:20:10
Balshaïa Kroutaïa Gouba,

•

02:17:21:18
02:17:23:20
Malaïa Kroutaïa Gouba,

•

02:17:25:16
02:17:27:06
Sharyjalgaï,

•

02:17:07:16
02:17:09:02
Medlyanka,

•

02:17:11:00
02:17:12:18
Angasolka,

•

02:17:14:18
02:17:16:04
Khabartui,

•

02:17:17:20
02:17:20:10
Bolshaya Krutaya Guba,

•

02:17:21:18
02:17:23:20
Malaya Krutaya Guba,

•

02:17:25:16
02:17:27:06
Sharyzhalgai,

•

02:17:28:18
02:17:30:22
Шарыжалгай Второй, Charijalgai Vtorói,

•

02:17:32:02
02:17:33:24
Шарыжалгай Третий, Charijalgai Tréti,

•

02:17:35:14
02:17:37:02
Шибартуй, Chibartui,

•

02:17:38:14
02:17:39:20
Бакланий, Bakláni,

•

02:17:42:04
02:17:43:14
Киркирей, Kirkirei,

•

02:17:45:22
02:17:47:08
Маритуй, Maritui,

•
02:17:28:18
02:17:30:22
Sharyjalgaï Vtaroï,

•
02:17:28:18
02:17:30:22
Sharyzhalgai Btoroi,

•
02:17:32:02
02:17:33:24
Sharyjalgaï Tretyi,

•
02:17:32:02
02:17:33:24
Sharyzhalgai Tretyi,

•
02:17:35:14
02:17:37:02
Shibartouï,

•
02:17:35:14
02:17:37:02
Shibartui,

•
02:17:38:14
02:17:39:20
Baklanyi,

•
02:17:38:14
02:17:39:20
Baklanyi,

•
02:17:42:04
02:17:43:14
Kirkirei,

•
02:17:42:04
02:17:43:14
Kirkirei,

•
02:17:45:22
02:17:47:08
Maritouï,

•
02:17:45:22
02:17:47:08
Maritui,

•

02:17:49:22
02:17:52:02

Большая Половинная, Bolchaia Polovínnaia,

•

02:17:54:06
02:17:56:14

Большая Пономаревка, Bolchaia Ponomariovka,

•

02:17:58:16
02:18:00:12

Малая Шумиха, Málaia Chumikha,

•

02:18:02:06
02:18:04:12

Большая Шумиха, Bolchaia Chumikha,

•

02:18:06:14
02:18:08:24

Большой Баранчик, Bolchoi Barántchik,

•

02:18:10:14
02:18:12:12

Малый Баранчик. Máli Barántchik.

•

02:17:49:22
02:17:52:02
Balshaïa Palavinnaïa,

•

02:17:54:06
02:17:56:14
Balshaïa Panamariovka,

•

02:17:58:16
02:18:00:12
Malaïa Shoumikha,

•

02:18:02:06
02:18:04:12
Balshaïa Shoumikha,

•

02:18:06:14
02:18:08:24
Balshoï Baranchick,

•

02:18:10:14
02:18:12:12
Malyi Baranchick.

•

02:17:49:22
02:17:52:02
Bolshaya Polovinnaya,

•

02:17:54:06
02:17:56:14
Bolshaya Ponomarevka,

•

02:17:58:16
02:18:00:12
Malaya Shumikha,

•

02:18:02:06
02:18:04:12
Bolshaya Shumikha,

•

02:18:06:14
02:18:08:24
Bolshoi Baranchick,

•

02:18:10:14
02:18:12:12
Malyi Baranchick.

•

02:18:16:18
02:18:22:04

Это не те 336 рек,
о которых я узнал в школе.

Estes não são os nomes dos 336 rios
que aprendi na escola.

•

02:18:23:18
02:18:28:18

Потому что теперь, говорят,
их 460.

Porque agora, dizem,
existem 460.

•

02:18:29:24
02:18:32:24

А из 460 рек

E destes 460,

•

02:18:33:20
02:18:37:12

только 277 имеют название.

só 227 têm nome.

•

02:18:39:06
02:18:42:02

Я думаю,
что остальные слишком малы,

Suponho porque todos os outros
são pequenos demais

•
02:18:16:18
02:18:19:16
Ceux-ci ne sont pas
les noms des 336 rivières

•
02:18:16:18
02:18:22:04
These are not the names
of the 336 rivers I learned in school.

•
02:18:19:18
02:18:22:12
que j'ai appris à l'école.

•
02:18:23:18
02:18:28:18
Parce que maintenant,
on dit qu'il y en a 460.

•
02:18:23:18
02:18:28:18
Because now, we are told,
there are 460.

•
02:18:29:24
02:18:32:24
Et sur ces 460 rivières,

•
02:18:29:24
02:18:32:24
And of these 460

•
02:18:33:20
02:18:37:12
seules 277 ont un nom.

•
02:18:33:20
02:18:37:12
only 277
have been named.

•
02:18:39:06
02:18:42:02
Je suppose que les autres
sont trop petites

•
02:18:39:06
02:18:42:02
I suppose because all the others
are too small

	• 02:18:42:06 02:18:44:20
чтобы иметь имя.	para merecerem um nome.
	• 02:18:49:18 02:18:52:08
У сказки о Хоридо и его жене	A história de Khorido e da sua mulher-cisne
	• 02:18:52:10 02:18:55:06
есть ещё один конец.	é também contada com um fim diferente.
	• 02:18:56:10 02:19:00:24
Женщина-лебедь попросила Хоридо вернуть ей оперение.	A mulher-cisne pediu a Khorido que lhe devolvesse as suas penas.
	• 02:19:01:10 02:19:03:22
Он принёс его из укрытия	Ele foi buscá-las ao seu esconderijo
	• 02:19:04:00 02:19:05:14
и отдал ей.	e deu-lhas.

•

02:18:42:08
02:18:44:20
pour qu'on leur
en donne un.

•

02:18:42:06
02:18:44:20
to be given a name.

•

02:18:49:18
02:18:52:08
L'histoire de Khorido
et de sa femme-cygne

•

02:18:49:18
02:18:52:08
The story of Khorido
and his swan-wife

•

02:18:52:10
02:18:55:06
est également racontée
avec une fin différente.

•

02:18:52:10
02:18:55:06
is also told with another ending.

•

02:18:56:10
02:19:00:24
La femme-cygne a demandé
à Khorido de lui rendre ses plumes.

•

02:18:56:10
02:19:00:24
The swan-woman requested
her feathers back from Khorido.

•

02:19:01:10
02:19:03:22
Il les sortit de l'endroit
où il les avait cachées

•

02:19:01:10
02:19:03:22
He fetched them
from his hiding place

•

02:19:04:00
02:19:05:14
et les lui a redonnées.

•

02:19:04:00
02:19:05:14
and gave them to her.

•

02:19:06:10
02:19:08:16

Она подержала оперение в руках,	Ela segurou-as nas mãos

•

02:19:09:10
02:19:10:08

а потом	e depois

•

02:19:10:14
02:19:12:16

вернула ему.	devolveu-as a Khorido.

•

02:19:14:02
02:19:17:10

Заглянув в глаза Хоридо,	E quando ela olhou para os olhos de Khorido,

•

02:19:17:16
02:19:20:18

она увидела, что они наполнились слезами.	viu que eles se tinham enchido de lágrimas.

•

02:19:23:14
02:19:26:12

А когда Хоридо посмотрел ей в глаза,	E quando Khorido olhou nos olhos dela,

•
02:19:06:10
02:19:08:16
Elle les a gardées dans les mains,

•
02:19:06:10
02:19:08:16
She held them in her hands,

•
02:19:09:10
02:19:10:08
puis, au bout d'un moment,

•
02:19:09:10
02:19:10:08
and then,

•
02:19:10:14
02:19:12:16
elle les lui a rendues.

•
02:19:10:14
02:19:12:16
she returned them to him.

•
02:19:14:02
02:19:17:10
Et lorsqu'elle a regardé
dans les yeux de Khorido,

•
02:19:14:02
02:19:17:10
And when she looked
into Khorido's eyes,

•
02:19:17:16
02:19:20:18
elle a vu qu'ils s'étaient remplis
de larmes.

•
02:19:17:16
02:19:20:18
she saw they had filled with tears.

•
02:19:23:14
02:19:26:12
Et quand Khorido a regardé
dans les siens,

•
02:19:23:14
02:19:26:12
And when Khorido
looked into her eyes,

•

02:19:27:06
02:19:30:12

он увидел, что они тоже
были полны слёз.

viu que também os dela
se tinham enchido de lágrimas.

•
02:19:27:06
02:19:30:12
il a vu qu'eux aussi
s'étaient remplis de larmes.

•
02:19:27:06
02:19:30:12
he saw that hers too
were filled with tears.

ГОЛОС ЗА КАДРОМ	VOZ
ЮРИЙ СТЕПАНОВ	Iúri Stepánov
ПЕРЕВОД	TRADUÇÃO
ЕЛЕНА ФИАЛКО	Elena Fialko – Tradução russa
	João Penalva – Tradução portuguesa
МОНТАЖ	PÓS-PRODUÇÃO
ДЭВИД ДОУСОН	David Dawson
СУБТИТРЫ	LEGENDAGEM
ПОЛИГОН ФИЛМЗ, ПАРИЖ	Polygone Films, Paris
ПРОИЗВОДСТВО ПРИ ПОДДЕРЖКЕ	APOIO DE
ФРАК ЛАНГЕДОК-РУССИОН, ФРАНЦИЯ	Frac Languedoc-Roussillon, França
АВТОР СЦЕНАРИЯ И РЕЖИССЁР	ESCRITO E REALIZADO POR
ЖОАО ПЕНАЛВА	João Penalva

Глубокая признательность за помощь
Ами Барак, Вере Папак, Максиму Тимофееву, М.Т.Х. Скотт, Нобухиро Таджима, Сюзанн Галер, Фернанде Роза, Фернанду Гарсиа

AGRADECIMENTOS
Ami Barak, Susanne Gahler, Fernand Garcia, Vera Papas, Fernanda Rosa, M.T.H. Scott, Nobuhiro Tajima, Maxim Timofeyev

VOIX

Youri Stepanov

TRADUCTION

Elena Fialko – Traduction russe

Caroline Reffay – Traduction française

POST-PRODUCTION

David Dawson

SOUS-TITRAGE

Polygone Films, Paris

AVEC LE SUPPORT DU

Frac Languedoc-Roussillon, France

ÉCRIT ET RÉALISÉ PAR

João Penalva

REMERCIEMENTS

Ami Barak, Susanne Gahler, Fernand Garcia, Vera Papas, Fernanda Rosa, M.T.H. Scott, Nobuhiro Tajima, Maxim Timofeyev

VOICE

Yuri Stepanov

TRANSLATION

Elena Fialko – Russian translation

English original text – João Penalva

POST-PRODUCTION

David Dawson

SUBTITLES

Polygone Films, Paris

SUPPORT

Frac Languedoc-Roussillon, France

WRITTEN AND DIRECTED BY

João Penalva

WITH THANKS TO

Ami Barak, Susanne Gahler, Fernand Garcia, Vera Papas, Fernanda Rosa, M.T.H. Scott, Nobuhiro Tajima, Maxim Timofeyev

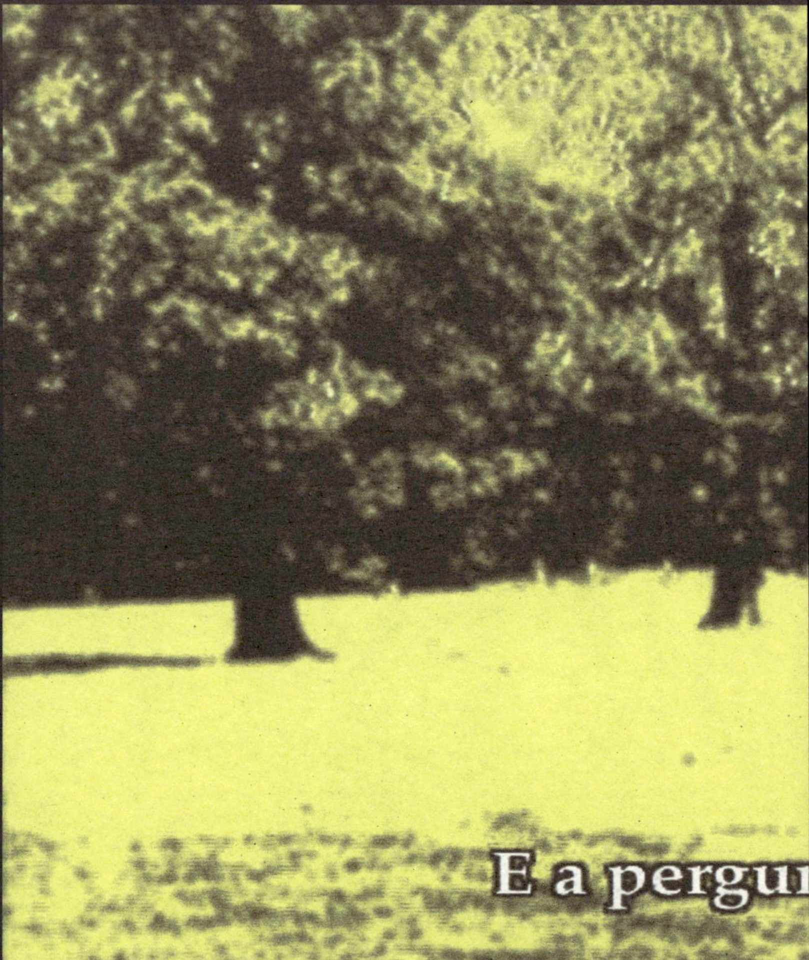

E a pergun

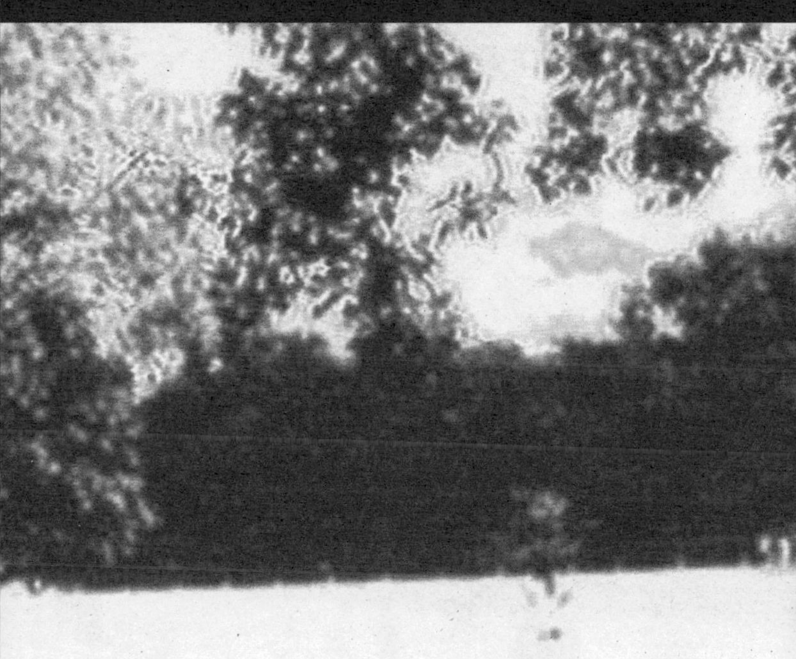

a dele era:

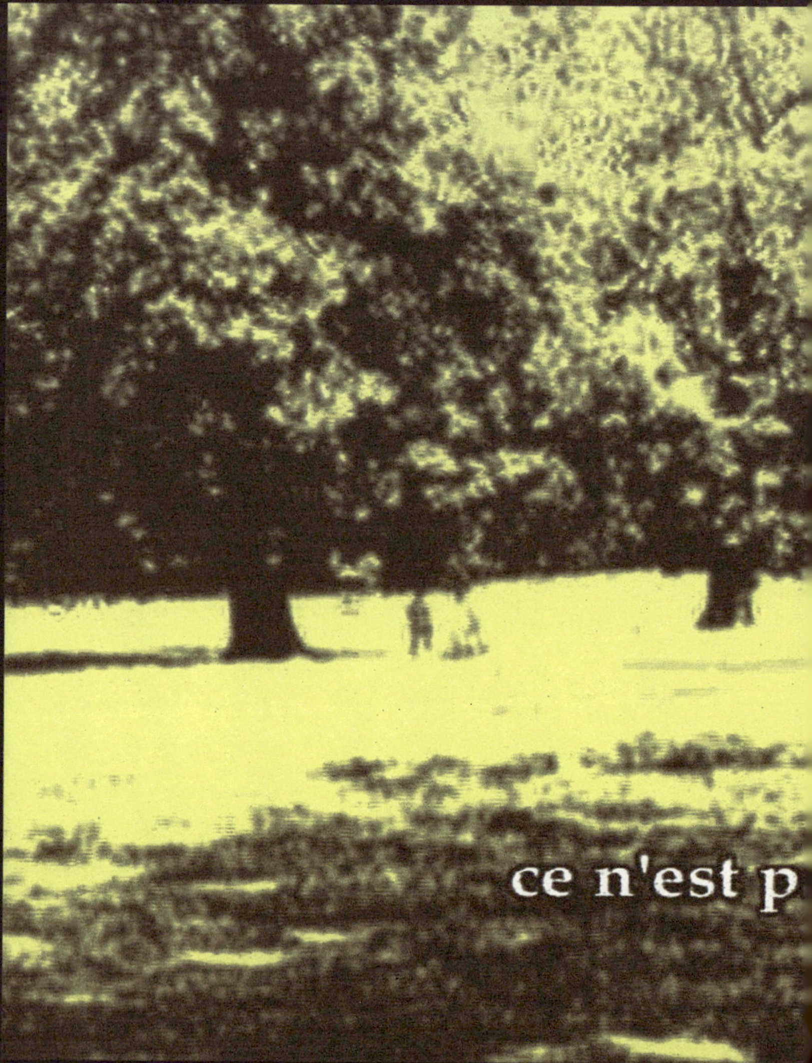

ce n'est p

ma voix.

Bolshaya Z

enovskaya,

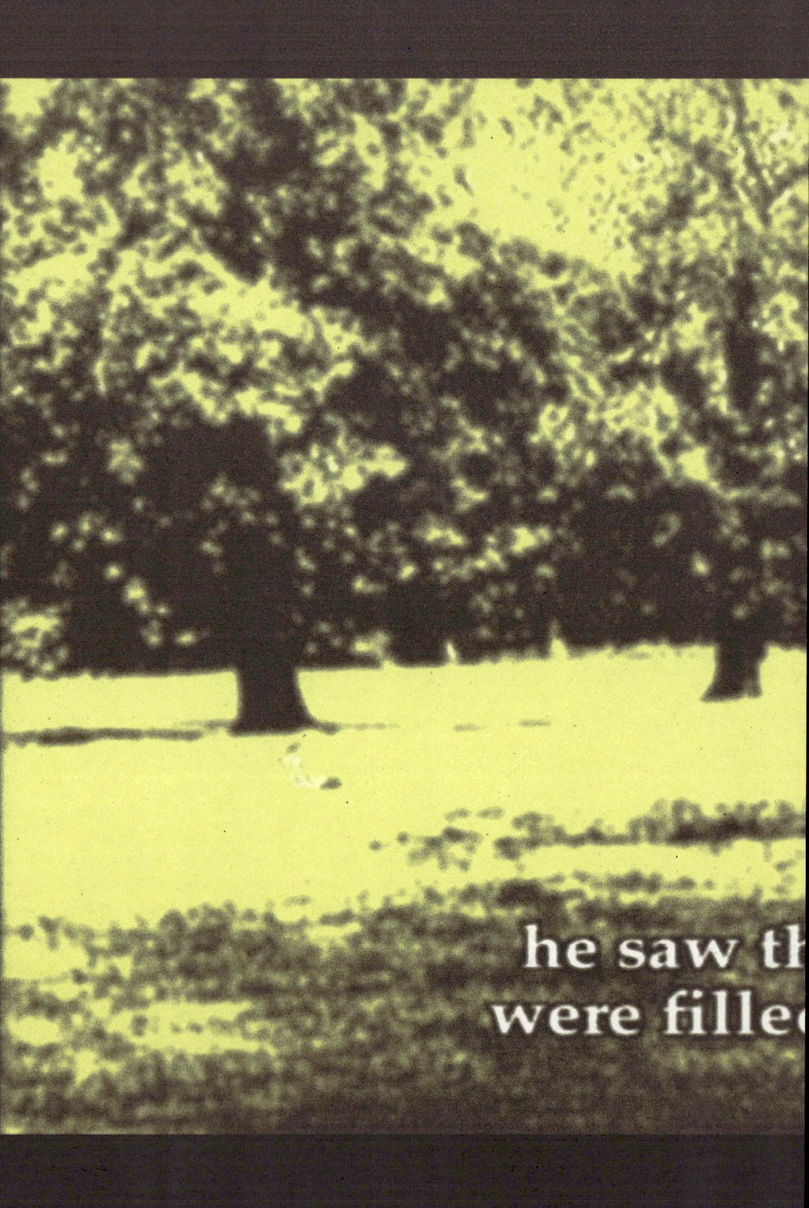
he saw th
were fille

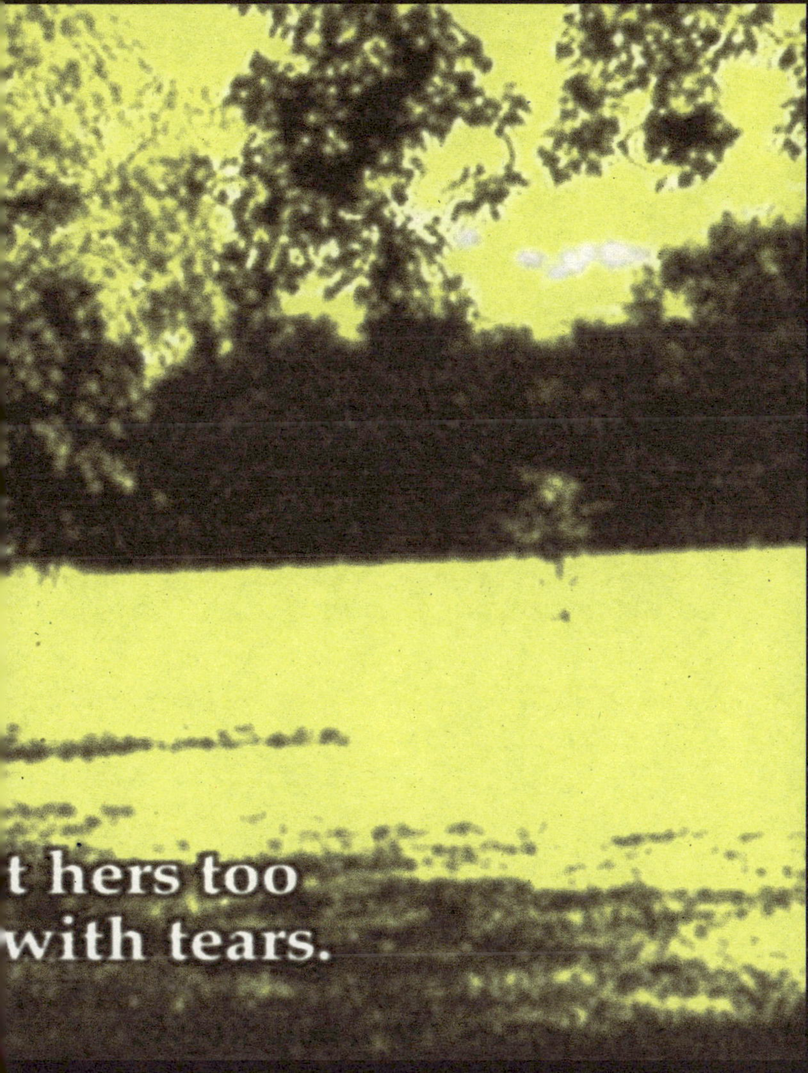

t hers too
with tears.